# NO LONGER REJECTED

To Kelly,
There is freedom
in Christ!

James Brown Jr.

D1260764

# NO LONGER REJECTED

## A Woman's Journey from Rejection to Freedom

## Janice Broyles

CROSSLINK
PUBLISHING

No Longer Rejected: A Women's Journey From Rejection To Freedom

D CrossLink Publishing
www.crosslinkpublishing.com

ISBN 978-1-63357-065-8

Library of Congress Control Number: 2016932011

All Scriptures are taken from the Holy Bible, King James Version (Public Domain).

*This book is dedicated
in loving memory to my mother,
Sharon Claire (Jones) Giertz*

*Until We Meet Again ...*

# TABLE OF CONTENTS

*For thou hast possessed my reins:*

*thou hast covered me in
my mother's womb.*

*I will praise thee; for I am fearfully and
wonderfully made:*

*marvelous are thy works; and that my soul
knoweth right well.*

*~Psalm 139: 13–14*

# Introduction

I stared at the empty signature line, not quite registering what it meant.

"You didn't sign it," I said, looking up at my administrator.

"Right," he said, shifting his posture and eyeing the door. "You see, after discussing it with the superintendent, we both agreed that we wouldn't be able to sign for you."

Still not registering the message behind the words, I pushed, "But you have to. I can't send in my application for Michigan Teacher-of-the-Year if I don't have yours and the superintendent's consent."

Unable to look me in the eye, my principal sighed, shrugged, and said simply, "You're not who we'd want to represent the district."

"Why not?" I asked, my brain not wanting to connect the dots. "I was nominated! This could give the district $50,000 dollars! I'd be up against only five other teachers! I stand a really good chance!"

And there it was. The moment it hit me. The moment I understood what he was saying without saying it. *You're not who we'd want to represent the district.*

*We think so little of you, you're not even worth the district receiving much-needed money.*

*You're not good enough.*

*You're not worth it.*

The tears came, though I wish they hadn't. Moments like these I wish I could be strong enough to stand up for myself. To not place my value and worth on someone else's opinion. I wanted to ask questions, but I already knew the answers.

No words came, and eventually he quietly said, "I'm sorry, Janice," before exiting my classroom.

In just a few minutes, someone had come into my life and took what should have been an honor and made it an insult. Not just an insult, but a rejection.

\* \* \*

In a perfect world there wouldn't be rejections. Everyone would feel loved, appreciated, and valued. Isn't that what rejection is? An absence of value? A struggle of worth?

Unfortunately we live in anything but a perfect world. We live in a world that places emphasis and importance on the superficial. This especially holds true for us women. What's on the outside takes center stage while our inner self deteriorates into a starved entity, craving any bone that can be thrown our way:

- We don't want to beg for attention, but we do.
- We don't want to compromise our beliefs and standards for flattery and lies, but we do.
- We don't want to feel the heavy weight of depression or the shackles of despair, but we do.

But that's inside. No one has to see that. Just as long as our smiles hide our flaws, our heels give us confidence, and our appearance creates our fantasy. Meanwhile our hearts break and our self-worth disappears. The more we rely on others' approval and acceptance, the more vulnerable we become.

But someone does see. He sees you and knows you by name. Jesus says in the Gospel of Luke:

> *Are not five sparrows sold for two farthings, and not one*
> *of them is forgotten before God? But even the very hairs*
> *on your head are all numbered. Fear not therefore: ye are of*
> *more value than many sparrows.*
> *Luke 12:6–7*

Yet, we readily believe a lie. We have it thrown at us from multiple outlets: advertising, the news, television and movies, the books we read, the catchy songs on the radio. Many of them broadcasting:

- Outward appearance reigns supreme.
- Divorce is just a part of life.
- Commitment is overrated.
- If it feels good, do it.
- Life is not sacred.
- Money and possessions create happiness.

All of these popular cultural ideals perpetuate a cycle of events and emotions that are completely contrary to God's design. Heartache, jealousy, bitterness, fear, loneliness, discontent, and anxiety continue to rob the life we were meant to live. And all of these emotions stem, ultimately, from rejection. From not feeling good enough.

This book challenges the cycle of rejection that bombards us, and it also reminds us that our ultimate worth and value can be found in Jesus Christ. Rejection and inadequacy were never part of God's initial design, and throughout Scripture, story after story highlights a loving God reaching for His people, reminding them that in His arms contentment, peace, and faithfulness are waiting.

Take a walk with me then through several stories of the Bible that focus on women facing rejection—from their communities, from their peer groups, from their family members, from the opposite sex—and see how God uses each of their situations for His ultimate purpose.

Rejection stings. It hurts deep inside. It has for me, many times over.

We can take rejection and bury it deep, allowing it to take root and grow into the vicious cycle of negative emotions, or we can lean on our Heavenly Father and give it to Him. Ultimately that's what I did.

And I've never looked back.

# Part I:
# Rejected!

*The Lord is close to the brokenhearted
and saves those who are
crushed in spirit.*

*~Psalm 34:18*

# CHAPTER ONE

## *What Did I Do Wrong?*

Do you remember the first time you experienced rejection? I do not necessarily recommend dwelling on past events, especially negative ones, but this memory seems to be easy for most of us to recall.

I remember distinctly the first time I ever felt rejected. A little girl in our church had turned six and her mother had decided to throw her a party. All the girls from the Sunday school class had been invited. Other than me. At least that's what I heard.

Interestingly enough, I would have never discovered the birthday party in the first place if my mother would have handled the situation better. Or more quietly. One Sunday morning after church, my mother came to the classroom to retrieve me. One look and I knew Mom wasn't happy. She snatched my arm and dragged me out of the room. My little mind worked frantically trying to figure out what I might have done to upset her.

That's when the confrontation began.

We had just turned the corner when the mother of the other little girl tried to walk past. My mother stepped in front of her. "Why isn't Janice invited to the birthday party?" My mother was never one to beat around the bush.

The woman glanced down at me, then smiled at my Mom. "I'm sorry, Sharon. We could only invite a few."

"*All* the other girls are invited," my mother countered.

At this point, the hall had become crowded, and I realized that Mom had attracted some attention. I tugged at her arm to leave.

I don't recall any more of the embarrassing conversation, but I do remember sitting in the car on the way home. Mom ranted almost the entire way about how when we have a party we wouldn't invite that family, and that I shouldn't feel bad. But I did. Mom was upset, so I should be upset. She cried, so I cried.

Little did I realize I would struggle with rejection for the rest of my life.

\* \* \*

For many of us women, understanding rejection doesn't take a lot of science. Not when we've been rejected. One definition I found interesting says that rejection is "to discard as useless or unsatisfactory."\*

Have you ever felt discarded? It could have been something as simple as a boy walking away from you to shower some other girl with his attention. It could also be something deeply rooted, such as years of pining for your father's attention and love but him never being around, whether physically or emotionally.

Rejection, at its core, is a struggle of worth. It says we aren't good enough; we're not worth loving; we're not worth caring about; we're not worth the next job or promotion; we're not worth fighting for.

None of those statements are true, especially when it comes to our Heavenly Father:

> *My grace is sufficient for you,*
> *for my power is made perfect in weakness.*
> *II Corinthians 12:9*

Yet, it seems easier to believe I'm not worth anything than to believe that my worth is of great value. But here's a news flash, God's Word doesn't lie:

> *Who can find a virtuous woman?*
> *For her place is far above rubies.*
> *Proverbs 31:10*

"Tell that to the person who rejected me!" you might counter. "They didn't act like I was above the dirt beneath their shoe, let alone some priceless gem!"

I get it. Truly, I do. Inadequacy is a powerful emotion, and one that our enemy uses relentlessly to keep us from living out our purpose in Christ. Thus, it is an internal battle that we must win. In order to do that, we have to come to terms with the "Why" behind it happening in the first place.

The question that is normally asked (at least it's what *I* normally ask) is: why did it happen to me? Other variations include (but are certainly not limited to):

- What did I do to deserve this?
- If I had tried harder, could I have been successful and avoided rejection?
- What can I change to make them like me?
- Am I unlikable? Unlovable?
- Will I ever be good enough?

The challenge with asking these questions is that it places the blame on the one who had to face and endure the rejection. This is not to assume that we do not bring negative circumstances upon ourselves through bad decisions and negative actions or reactions, but many times we are rejected for reasons outside of our control, or for reasons that are not logical, or we are simply rejected without ever knowing why.

Even though the battlefield of rejection is oftentimes played out with spoken words or deliberate actions as weapons, our wounds are internal. We might lash out occasionally, but usually we hide them so that no one will see the fatal blows to our heart. A close look at our society shows that these feelings can develop into self-loathing. And it affects us, changing the way we view our lives and the way we raise our children.

# CHAPTER TWO

## *Why Did God Let This Happen?*

After graduating from the University of Michigan in December of 1999, I pursued a career as soon as I had the degree in my hand. Every day I would mail out resumes. From Sterling Heights to the West side of Detroit, I lined up interviews over the entire Metro area. I would practice my interview in front of the mirror, dress in my nicest business suit, and review my portfolio.

And I would pray. As soon as a school district would call me, I'd begin my prayer routine. It went something like this: "Please, please, please, please, *please*, give me this job. *Please!*" I would walk around the house, naming it and claiming it. Out of the dozen interviews over the greater Detroit area, surely God would hand me the perfect one.

Nope.

I didn't land one of them.

I went through the entire winter and spring of 2000 without a teaching job lined up for fall. June came, and I was officially worried.

That's when I received the call for an interview from Rochester Hills Community Schools. This was it. THE job. I had worked for Rochester Hills as a substitute teacher and wanted a teaching position there in the worst way. Man, you want to talk about prayer time! Granted I was doing most of the talking, and most of what I said revolved around the word, "Please," but I was fairly certain this interview was from God, and the position was mine.

The interview couldn't have gone any better. I answered the questions just as I had practiced. I smiled and was engaging. They smiled back. At the end of the interview when I shook their hands, the head principal shook my hand last and said, "You *will* hear from us."

I walked out of that interview grinning from ear to ear. I thanked God as soon as I got to the car. I told my husband and my friends that God had given me my dream job.

Two days later I received a call from the head principal at Rochester Hills Community Schools. She told me it was such a difficult decision, but they had decided on someone else.

I hung up the phone and felt utterly defeated. At first I cried, asking God "Why?" Then I became angry. "Why are you doing this to me?" I yelled up at the ceiling. This had been the thirteenth school district to say no.

When I called my friend to vent, she quickly put me in my place. "So, you're angry at God because He's not giving you what you want, when you want it? It's easy to trust Him when everything is going your way, but can you trust Him when it isn't?"

Needless to say I hung up the phone extremely annoyed and even more convicted. I had to make a decision. Would I allow the rejections of all those school districts to defeat me? Or would I trust in God to see me through?

At the end of July I received a full-time job offer 200 miles north of the Metro area. God directed us where He wanted us. And that Rochester Hills job? The following year, I read that the district had to lay off all the new hires from the previous years because of funding issues. Now looking back, I can see how God's hand was on the entire situation.

His will is not to hurt us. His will is perfect and good. We may have to deal with rejection, but trust me, God's got it all figured out.

### Rejection Was Not God's Plan

*Now the serpent was more subtle than any beast of the field which the* Lord *God had made. And he said unto the woman, Yea, hath God said, Ye shall not eat of every tree of the garden? And the woman said unto the serpent, We may eat of the fruit of the trees of the garden: But of the fruit of the tree which is in the midst of the garden, God hath said, Ye shall not eat of it, neither shall ye touch it, lest ye die. And the serpent said unto the woman, Ye shall not surely die: For God doth know that in the day ye eat thereof, then your eyes shall be opened, and ye shall be as gods, knowing good and evil. And when the woman saw that the tree was good for food, and that it was pleasant to the eyes, and a tree to be desired to make one wise, she took of the fruit thereof, and did eat, and gave also unto her husband with her; and he did eat. And the eyes of them both were opened, and they knew that they were naked; and they sewed fig leaves together, and made themselves aprons. And they heard the voice of the* Lord *God walking in the garden in the cool of the day: and Adam and his wife hid themselves from the presence of the* Lord *God amongst the trees of the garden. And the* Lord *God called unto Adam, and said unto him, Where art thou?*

*Genesis 3:1–9*

Eve just *had* to eat the fruit. We can't even blame Adam because he took a bite after Eve did. Simply put, Eve had been beguiled. She had believed a lie. One that told her that God was holding out on her. God had secrets and He wasn't sharing, or so said the serpent. Yes, it was a bad decision on Eve's part, but consider the consequences of that decision. She and her husband were evicted. Cast out from the garden and sentenced to a life of toil and hard labor. Can you imagine the conversation between Adam and Eve? I doubt that evening's dinner was enjoyable.

Even though I sympathize over their situation—and try very hard not to judge—it's important to note that none of that was God's plan. He created them to develop a relationship with Him. Part of relationship is choice; choosing to be with someone is much more intimate than being forced to be with Him. By listening to the enemy, Eve altered the rest of existence. Not the best thing to being remembered for, is it?

Rejection then, from the very beginning, grew from a lie. *It is the result of sin.*

What is comforting, though, is that God had only planned on us receiving his best. Agony and despair were not a part of his formula. And God loves us so much that He already had a plan of action in order to reconcile us back to Him. He doesn't like being separated from us. Sin created a chasm between us and God, and God's own son shed his innocent blood to bridge that gap. When we live a life of defeat and dissatisfaction as a result of past hurts and rejections, we remove ourselves from Him, despite everything He's done to bring us closer.

We can't make the same mistake Eve made and listen to the voice of the enemy.

### Rejection Does Not Mean Failure

*And Naomi said unto her two daughters in law,*
*Go, return each to her mother's house: the LORD deal kindly with you,*
*as ye have dealt with the dead, and with me.*
*The LORD grant you that ye may find rest,*
*each of you in the house of her husband. Then she kissed them;*
*and they lifted up their voice, and wept.*
*And they said unto her, Surely we will return with*
*thee unto thy people.*
*And Naomi said, Turn again, my daughters: why will ye go with*
*me? are there yet any more sons in my womb, that they may be your*
*husbands? Turn again, my daughters, go your way; for I am too old*
*to have an husband. If I should say, I have hope, if I should have an*
*husband also to night, and should also bear sons; Would ye tarry*
*for them till they were grown? Would ye stay for them from having*
*husbands? Nay, my daughters; for it grieveth me much for your*
*sakes that the hand of the LORD is gone out against me.*
*And they lifted up their voice, and wept again: and Orpah kissed her*
*mother in law; but Ruth clave unto her. And she said, Behold, thy*
*sister in law is gone back unto her people, and unto her gods: return*
*thou after thy sister in law.*
*And Ruth said, Entreat me not to leave thee, or to return from*
*following after thee: for whither thou goest, I will go; and where thou*
*lodgest, I will lodge: thy people shall be my people, and thy God my*
*God …*
*Ruth 1:8–16*

Sometimes people reject us by saying no. That does not necessarily mean that the door is shut forever. Naomi, from the book of Ruth, had lost her husband and then recently lost her two sons. She would naturally be mourning the loss of her family. When she decided to head back to Judah, her family's homeland, her two daughters-in-law, Ruth and Orpah, packed up to go with her. At some point in the journey, Naomi stopped and told the two younger women to go home to their mothers' house. The Bible says that she wished them well, and even cried with them, but none of that changed her mind. She wanted them to go back to Moab.

The Scripture shows us how the two young women handled Naomi's decision. Orpah took Naomi's no and turned around and went home. Ruth did not. Ruth pushed past the initial rejection and insisted on going with Naomi. The Bible says she "clave unto her." Ruth ended up marrying Boaz and was used by God to be the bloodline of Jesus.

When faced with rejection, or someone telling you "No," don't immediately assume failure. How many successful authors and entrepreneurs heard "No," yet continued on the path they thought they were meant for? Sometimes that "No" means God is redirecting you, and sometimes a "No" simply means that you need to press on. Seek God and trust Him to direct you because in his eyes, rejection doesn't mean failure.

### Rejection is Not the End

> *And he said, I will certainly return unto thee according to the time of life; and, lo, Sarah thy wife shall have a son.*
>
> *And Sarah heard it in the tent door, which was behind him. Now Abraham and Sarah were old and well stricken in age; and it ceased to be with Sarah after the manner of women. Therefore Sarah laughed within herself, saying, After I am waxed old shall I have pleasure, my lord being old also?*
>
> *And the LORD said unto Abraham, Wherefore did Sarah laugh, saying, Shall I of a surety bear a child, which am old? Is any thing too hard for the LORD? At the time appointed I will return unto thee, according to the time of life, and Sarah shall have a son.*
>
> *Genesis 18: 10–14*

When God is given control, rejection will not have the final say. This can be seen in several Biblical accounts such as Sarah, in Genesis 18, and Elizabeth, in the book of Luke.

Both women felt the rejection of their communities because of their barren wombs. Both must have had feelings of dejection and doubt watching other women bearing what Sarah and Elizabeth only longed for. Yet God knew exactly what He was doing and, in the end, Sarah and Elizabeth delivered a promised child of God.

Sometimes a rejection, or a "No," is really a "not right now." Trust that God's perfect timing will be fulfilled.

# Part II:

# You're Not Alone!

*Yea, though I walk through the
valley of the shadow of death,
I will fear no evil, for you are with me;
your rod and your staff, they comfort me.*

*~Psalm 23:4*

# CHAPTER THREE

## *Rejected by Religious Leaders*
## *Mary Magdalene*

I was the golden child of my church. I even have the awards to prove it.

Camper-of-the-year at church camp. I beat out a little over 200 campers. The reward honored a camper who reflected Jesus and whose heart yearned for a future with the Lord. I guess I demonstrated that more than the others. Yay, me.

Student-of-the-year at our church school. I won the most awards during that end-of-the-year ceremony than anyone else. Not that I'm bragging.

Teen-of-the-year at church. I won that award twice. Once as a fourteen-year-old, and then I won again as a seventeen-year-old. For the record, I think I'm the only one who won that award more than once.

Sheaves for Christ Scholarship recipient. I had the honor of winning this notable scholarship through my church denomination's international organization. It would pay for the first two years of Bible College. This had been a major honor.

When I packed up and headed to Bible College, I thought I was ready for the next chapter of my overachieving, people-pleasing life.

Nine months later I would be kicked out of that Bible College. Heartbroken, scared, and ashamed.

What happened?

Simple: I met a boy.

I understood the rules of the college. No dating freshman year. No dating members of the foundational church's youth. And no touching. Definitely none of that. But that didn't matter when the young man expressed interest in me. I had been the awkward girl through most of my teenage years, so I fell hard for the fellow from the church. He wasn't a college student, so the rules didn't apply to him. So, what did I do? I learned to date around the rules. This involved a lot of love letters and secret meet-ups, especially during the night. Since I had been on the ground floor of the dorms, getting in and out of my window had been easy.

Getting caught was bad. Every church girl's worst nightmare.

Sitting in the college president's office with the boy's parents and several members of the College Board was even worse. Being called a liar and other cruel words by the president, who happened to be a minister I respected and admired, nearly brought me to my knees.

As I sat there and tried to defend myself, completely betrayed by the boy and his parents, I was wholly heartbroken, not knowing what to do with the feelings of despair and rejection. To make matters worse, what they accused me of I did not do, but I no longer had the credibility for these elite church officials to believe me. Why should they believe a girl who had been deceiving them for the past several months?

At some point during that meeting, it dawned on me that God had to be angry with me, too. And if these people who were the voice of God on earth didn't believe the truth, then neither would He.

I was told to leave and to get my heart right with God. But for the first time in this church girl's life, I didn't know how to accomplish that.

\* \* \*

The church is more than just a building. The body of Christ, which is all of us, is the church. Have you ever wondered if you're the little toe? Insignificant. Tucked in a shoe. Usually forgotten. Well, I have.

Rejection from church leaders impacts us women in profound and deeply wounding ways. This rejection from those we usually admire and trust can lead to guilt and shame, as well as a disconnect from God. If these ministers condemn me, then does God condemn me, too?

The church should be a place of refuge and healing. When its people are the ones throwing the stones, those of us who've been accused don't know where to run. The following months after being kicked out of Bible College nearly pushed me into my spiritual grave.

Condemnation points a finger. That, in and of itself, can lead to isolation.

Even if the individual's bad choices were entirely her doing.

## Mary Magdalene

> *And the scribes and Pharisees brought unto him a*
> *woman taken in adultery;*
> *and when they had set her in the midst,*
> *They say unto him, Master, this woman was taken*
> *in adultery, in the very act. Now Moses in the law*
> *commanded us, that such should be stoned:*
> *but what sayest thou?*
> *John 8:3–5*

Mary Magdalene, considered by many to be the accused woman in John chapter 8, had quite the reputation. She had to have endured a barrage of past abuse because Luke specifically states in his eighth chapter that she had been set free of "seven devils." An outcast with a dark past is not the type of woman that the church necessarily wants. The religious leaders of Jesus' time felt the same way. They didn't understand how Jesus could be so accepting and forgiving of a woman who was guilty of so much.

Her internal battles we will never know—although I'm sure they might resemble ours more than we'd think—but her external surroundings were hostile.

Being rejected privately is one thing, but being rejected publicly, and by the leaders of the community no less, is enough to break any person. To make matters worse, this woman in John chapter 8 bears the guilt alone, not the man involved. The religious leaders acted out against her, making the public rejection that much more isolating.

How did it happen?

- This woman caught in adultery was *guilty*.
- The religious leaders discovered her … *in the act*.

- The religious leaders proceeded to drag her out from wherever she had been into the streets for *all to see.*
- Her sin was *exposed.*
- Instead of encouragement from the church, she received *death threats.*
- The stones were *already* in their hands.

> *In short, this woman endured humiliation in public at the hands of the religious community.*

What do you do when the men and women of God you respect suddenly turn on you? What do you do when they take a private situation and make it public? Sometimes, as women, we bear the guilt and shame when things go wrong. When a girl gets pregnant, it's her reputation that suffers often, not the fellow who put her in that position. In my own situation, I was the one called into the office and reprimanded, not the young man. I had been kicked out, but he became a Bible College student there the following year.

Many of us have to deal with the aftermath of disintegrated relationships and shattered hopes. When we are vulnerable we need the church and our leaders the most. I had been so heartsick over the events that I turned inward, closely guarding my feelings. For whatever reason, I couldn't penetrate the wall that seemed to separate me from God. If these ministers rejected me, then so did God.

That summer I fell down the rabbit hole. Back at home, I had other friends who were also disillusioned and ostracized by the church. We would cruise the streets looking for guys and parties. One thing about alcohol is that it numbs you. I could drink enough of it and forget that I was hated by the church community.

Thankfully, someone stopped me from the self-destructive path. That someone was my mother.

A praying woman, she refused for me to forget the calling she saw on my life. Instead of arguing with me, she prayed. She loved on me. She let me cry on her shoulders. She supported me. I remember one evening I sat down at the kitchen table and rested my head in my hands. My friend would be picking me up soon for another wild night, but I was tired. And miserable.

All my mother did was rest her hand on my shoulder. "Why are you running?" she asked quietly. "Don't you see that God doesn't need those people to believe in you? He already believes in you."

"But I messed up," I had said. "I broke the rules."

"Did you confess your sins to God? Isn't He faithful to forgive?"

"Yeah, but I feel like there's this wall between me and Him. I let Him down, too."

"Who built the wall?"

I wish I could say I stayed home that evening, but I didn't. However, when my mother asked me to attend a Ladies' Retreat with her the next weekend, I accepted. That weekend God moved upon me in the most powerful way that I had yet encountered at that point in my life.

On my knees, my hands in the air, tears falling from my face, I peeled off the shame and guilt that had clothed me from the rejection of that religious counsel. Instead, at that moment, I felt God's peace and love. I realized then that *I had built the wall*. I had built it brick-by-brick with rejection being the foundation. I had found myself guilty, and I thought that because of the rejection from so many religious leaders, I had to wear that guilt and rejection like a badge to warn people not to get close to the sinner.

When Mary Magdalene encountered Jesus, the same thing happened. Jesus not only forgave her, but He also set her free. He showed her, and all of us through her, that His thoughts are not the same as our thoughts. He looked right at the scribes and Pharisees in John chapter 8 and said words that have echoed through time:

*He that is without sin, cast the first stone.*

In both instances, in Mary's life and mine, Jesus restored life and purpose.

The bondage of rejection as a result of the misguided words and actions of the religious community is the enemy's way of warping our view of God and His body. Before walking away from the fellowship of believers, remind yourself:

- Look to God as the author and finisher of your faith, not other people.
- When you repent, God no longer remembers your sin.
- Don't believe any words that do not align with Scripture.
- Forgive them. Just as Jesus forgave us, forgive those in the church who have hurt and rejected you.
- Don't build a wall. This means you have to forgive yourself as well.

### Final thoughts

If Mary Magdalene hadn't listened to Jesus, if she had continued to wallow in her sin and the rejection thrown her way by the religious elite and community, she would have missed most of Jesus' ministry. She would have missed sitting at his feet and learning the keys to the kingdom. She would have missed the observance of his ultimate sacrifice. No matter how crushing it was for her to see her gentle master and Savior die on the cross, she still stood beside Jesus' mother and was there to care for the body.

If she would have allowed rejection to continue to steer the course of her life, she wouldn't have been at the tomb to see the angel. She wouldn't have been *the first one* to hear the words that Jesus had risen. (Matthew 28:4–6) Even better than that, because she made a conscientious decision to cast off her old life and follow Christ, she was *the first one* to see the resurrected Jesus.

Don't allow the rejection of different church members or religious leaders to dissuade you from a relationship with Jesus. He doesn't build the wall that stands between us and Him. We do. So tear down the wall rejection built inside of you, and run to your Savior who is waiting with open arms.

# CHAPTER FOUR

## *Rejected by Her Husband*
## *Leah*

The moment I walked through the door, I sensed it. Mom stood at the counter sobbing so hard no words could come out of her mouth. I dropped my purse and ran over to her, wrapping my arms around her.

"It'll be okay," I remember saying. I had no idea what had happened, but I certainly hoped whatever happened would blow over.

Mom shoved me away, shaking her head. Barely able to get out any words, she managed to say the three words that rocked our family's world, "Your … dad … left…." She left the kitchen and shut the door to her bedroom where I could hear her wailing.

At the time, I felt completely blindsided. My parents had a far-from-perfect marriage, but they had celebrated their twenty-fifth anniversary not even a year before. Now looking back at it I can see the warning signs that as a nineteen-year-old, I wasn't mature enough or wise enough to understand.

I stumbled out of the house and made my way to the open field that sat between us and a mechanic's shop. I fell to my knees in the tall grass, wiping at my own tears. I didn't like seeing my mother so hurt. I had never seen her so distraught.

The questions then came in a hurry. Were his things still at the house? When would he take us on vacations? How would we spend Christmas? Where would he live? But the question that kept repeating itself was: why would Dad do this? If Dad had rejected Mom, then he must have rejected me and my siblings.

The following weeks and months became some of the worst of my life. My mother, normally a powerful pillar of our church, lost it. Her volatile emotions would take over more often than not. I'd hear her throwing things, breaking frames, yelling into the telephone, crying in the night. At one point, when Dad came to pick up some things, Mom stood outside with boxes and began throwing his items at him. I hid in my room with my sister, both of us crying as we watched the train wreck of our parents' marriage disintegrate and burn.

More than that, Mom would come to me and my younger sister and beg us not to have anything to do with our dad. In her eyes he hadn't only rejected her, but he also had rejected his children, too. I easily believed it, and I became angrier and angrier at my father for the pain and hurt he caused my mother and his children.

The grief it caused my mother took its toll on me. I decided not to go back for a third year of Bible College even though I loved the new college I had transferred to the year before. I worried about Mom being alone. I ended up enrolling in a local community college in order to stay home and be with her.

I watched as my mother struggled internally with insecurity and jealousy. How could such a wonderful woman of God allow the anguish of a broken heart destroy any chance of ever finding a fulfilling relationship in the future? My heart would become heavy the many times through the years she would call just needing me to remind her that she was loved and cared about. At other times, there were moments when she would turn manipulative and act out against me or my siblings because she was hurt, angry, and jealous at our time spent with our father.

"So, I guess you love him more, huh?"

Unfortunately, these words would inadvertently push us away.

I wish I could say that my mother was able to quickly move on from the rejection she felt in that August of 1994, but she struggled for years. My siblings and I had made peace with Dad, and he worked hard at continuing a relationship with us. That only hurt Mom all the more.

Holidays became nightmares. Any time my siblings and I would spend time with Dad, Mom would be a mess. Any time I would go visit my father and she found out about it, she'd call me either in tears or with a tone of accusation. At my wedding, she was nearly undone at the prospect of my father walking me down the aisle. I watched how—even though she was a strong prayer warrior and unwavering Christian—she let bitterness and unforgiveness plague her, simply because she had been unsuccessful at overcoming the rejection of feeling unloved.

My mother's feelings of rejection ruled her life for far too many years. And it still grieves me to this day.

\* \* \*

A wedding day is one of the most significant, memorable days in a bride's life. As young girls, my friends and I would dream of our weddings. Who would we marry? What would be the colors? What kind of flowers and bouquets? What songs would play?

After the wedding—once the people are gone, the music has stopped, and the honeymoon is over—we quickly learn there is no guarantee of happiness. Marriage trends in America are sobering. Half of all marriages end in divorce.* Less than half of US children actually live in a "traditional" family household.* Approximately 15 million of these children, as of 2013, live in fatherless homes.*

What happened to marriage? To happily ever after?

To make marriage breakups worse, 80 percent of divorces are not a mutually-agreed upon decision.* This means that divorce is normally desired by one person of the union, not both.* Simply put, one of the two in the marriage is going to suffer a broken heart and the pangs of rejection.

Even though brokenheartedness is not gender-exclusive, for women, the feeling of being unloved affects how we view ourselves and how we handle the world around us.

- Our guard comes up. This creates a lack of trust in future relationships.
- We question our worth. This leads to depression and self-pity.
- We become insecure. Our insecurities also affect our relationships with others.
- We become manipulative. We try to force others to say or do things to show their love for us, but it only brings on guilt, which pushes away the people we care about.
- We become jealous of each other, even sabotaging other women's happiness through gossip and criticism. (If we can't be happy, no one else can!)

For many of us the rejection seems insurmountable, especially when we feel cheated of all the time and investment we placed into the marriage. "I did all of this, and you're just going to up and leave?"

These feelings are understandable, but dwelling on them will only allow rejection and all its friends to take up residency in your heart. Finding peace, love, and acceptance in Jesus is the only way to truly break free from the deep wound of divorce or separation.

## Leah

> Now Laban had two daughters. The name of the older was Leah,
> and the name of the younger was Rachel. Leah's eyes were weak, but
> Rachel was beautiful in form and appearance. Jacob loved Rachel.
> And he said, "I will serve you seven years for your
> younger daughter Rachel."
> … So Jacob served seven years for Rachel, and they seemed to him
> but a few days because of the love he had for her. Then Jacob said
> to Laban, "Give me my wife that I may go in to her, for my time is
> completed." So Laban gathered together all the people of the place
> and made a feast.
> But in the evening he took his daughter Leah and brought her to
> Jacob, and he went in to her … And in the morning, behold, it was
> Leah! And Jacob said to Laban, "What is this you have done to me?
> Did I not serve with you for Rachel?
> Why then have you deceived me?"
> Laban said, "It is not so done in our country, to give the younger
> before the firstborn. Complete the week of this one, and we will give
> you the other also in return for serving me another seven years."
> Jacob did so, and completed her week. Then Laban gave him his
> daughter Rachel to be his wife … So Jacob went in to Rachel also,
> and he loved Rachel more than Leah,
> and served Laban for another seven years.
> Genesis 29:16–30

Poor Leah. How it must have felt to live with a sister who
was known throughout the land as a beauty. If that wasn't bad

enough, Leah's father forces her to trick Jacob into marriage. She knew how much Jacob loved Rachel. I'm sure those two lovebirds made their declarations long before the wedding day. And then Jacob was so distraught he left Leah after the first night (the Jewish custom was a seven-day wedding feast), furious at being tricked out of the agreement. Even though he eventually fulfilled the week-long wedding celebration, it was only at the promise that Rachel would be given to him at the end of that week and with another seven-year obligation.

My heart hurts thinking of the morning after the consummation of the marriage bed when Leah's veil was removed. Leah—another pawn of Laban's deception—probably had no choice to marry Jacob, no choice but to marry someone who had never and would never love her, at least not in the way he loved her sister.

We know she was unloved because God saw it and responded to it:

> *When the Lord saw Leah was hated,*
> *he opened up her womb.*
> *Genesis 29:31*

Even with the gift of children, she still longed for her husband's affection. This can be seen in the names of her children:

> *And Leah conceived, and bare a son, and she called his name*
> *Reuben: for she said, Surely the LORD hath looked upon my*
> *affliction; now therefore my husband will love me. And she*
> *conceived again, and bare a son; and said, Because the LORD*
> *hath heard I was hated, he hath therefore given me this son*
> *also: and she called his name Simeon. And she conceived*
> *again, and bare a son; and said, Now this time will my*
> *husband be joined unto me, because I have born him three*
> *sons: therefore was his name called Levi.*
> *Genesis 29:32–34*

Leah hoped that bearing a son would be enough for Jacob to show her some affection, and she continued longing for his love with baby number two and baby number three. She tried to accomplish what many of us have tried to accomplish in loveless marriages: an effort to manipulate love and affection by giving our spouses what we think they want. "If I do this for him, then he'll love me."

Though children should be considered a blessing from God, and definitely were in this case, Leah's turmoil is still clearly evident. She probably had to endure Jacob lavishing his adoration and attention on Rachel, even though it was Leah's womb that, in the beginning, provided him heirs.

The good news is that Leah did not allow rejection to rule her life. How so? Look at her change of attitude with her fourth son:

> *And she conceived again, and bare a son: and she said,*
> *Now will I praise the Lord: therefore she called his name*
> *Judah; and left bearing.*
> *Genesis 29:35*

Something happened between the third and fourth son. It must have dawned on her that she would never be able to change Jacob or his feelings for Rachel. However, she could still enjoy life with the blessings and provision God supplied to her. Choosing to praise is the best answer when dealing with rejection. Our eyes are off ourselves and our situation and how someone else hurt us, and we're focused on God.

### Final Thoughts

Feeling unloved through rejection, especially when we have devoted time and energy into making the relationship work, easily opens the door for despair and bitterness. Whether we're pining away for what we once had or we're longing to change someone whose heart was never as invested as ours, it's difficult to let the past go or to admit that our future hopes and plans with that person will never come to fruition. That doesn't mean that God no longer has a purpose for us. It doesn't mean that we are washed up. And it certainly doesn't mean that we're unloved.

> *For I am persuaded, that neither death, nor life, nor angels, nor principalities, nor powers, nor things present, nor things to come, Nor height, nor depth, nor any other creature, shall be able to separate us from the love of God, which is in Christ Jesus our Lord.*
> *Romans 8:38–39*

More than God loving us, He completely understands the struggle against rejection and all the negative feelings that come with it. We are not alone in our heartache. The New International Version of Isaiah 38:17 says:

> *Surely it was for my benefit that I suffered such anguish.*
> *In your love you kept me from the pit of destruction;*
> *you have put all my sins behind your back.*

Leah overcame the rejection in her life and learned to praise God anyway. You might say, "But Rachel ended up having children! And her children were favored by Jacob! How is that fair or right?"

Yes, it is true that Rachel was blessed by God (Remember, Rachel is not the bad guy in this story. She was another pawn of Laban's deception.), and yes, she had Jacob's love and favor, but God did not forget Leah. It was through Leah that sprang the lineage of Jesus Christ. Jesus was of the tribe of Judah, Leah's fourth son.

Isn't that amazing? We are loved and favored by the Most High. And his blessings can spring forth from any mess. We may be rejected by someone who we loved and cared for, but we will never be rejected or unloved by our spiritual bridegroom.

# CHAPTER FIVE

## *Rejected by Men*
## *Tamar*

Here's a confession: I've never been blonde, and I've never been thin. Those two ingredients were necessary to secure a boyfriend. At least that's what I wrote in my journal when I was twelve. Later, as a teenager, I grew tall enough that I thinned out some. Now when I look at pictures, I can't believe how young, fresh, and skinny I looked. But according to my doctors even back then, I needed to lay off the chips and doughnuts.

Unfortunately for me, I had several friends who fit the definition of pretty. At church camps, they quickly found boyfriends. Most of the time, boys would only talk to me to get to one of my friends. At school, I fared no better: none of the boys were interested in the chubby church girl.

To make matters worse, I had quite a few crushes. Most of the boys I liked I actually wrote about in my journal. (And yes, I still have that journal.) Interestingly, I pretty much crushed on all of my older brother's friends. For the record, not one of them showed interest in me.

Usually, my interactions with the older boys were limited. They would treat me kindly, but their attention never really landed on me. Since my brother and I were only a few years apart in age, I would usually tag along, including youth group activities and special services. As my friends and I grew up, the older boys started taking notice. Let me clarify: they started noticing my friends.

After church one evening, my friend and I stood in the hall discussing where the youth group should go out to eat. My brother's friend goes to walk by. All of a sudden—and I still have no idea why my friend decided to do this—my friend blurted across the hall, "Hey, Frank, guess who has a crush on you? Janice does!"

Frank looked uncomfortable, as did I. Actually, I was mortified.

As if that wasn't enough, my friend, yelled, "Why don't you two go out? You like her, don't you?"

The words "No way!" came out of his mouth, but it was his look of disgust that I remember the most.

Yes, I went home and wrote horrible things about him in my journal. Not that it made me feel any better. To add more hurt to the situation, that same friend of mine started dating Frank a few short months later.

I didn't really understand heartache, though, until I was old enough to want to start dating seriously. After my second year of Bible College, when I had made the decision to stay home and help my mother, I was definitely on the lookout for a serious relationship. No longer as awkward as I had been in my school years, I also had developed some confidence, or at least I played the part pretty well. I might have been burned by what happened with my first real boyfriend, but a year had passed and I wanted to try again.

As a young adult, I was very much aware of the sexual climate of the mid-nineties. The whole wait-until-marriage idea didn't seem as appealing as it did when I was in youth class five years prior. I began to feel different but for other reasons than just my weight and hair color. Being single and being a Christian doesn't always mix well. Managing self-control, especially when some good-looking man is whispering in your ear how beautiful you are, takes determination and the Holy Spirit to resist and stay pure.

One particular evening, after sharing how lonely I was to another one of my friends from church, he had the brilliant idea of setting me up with one of his friends from work. Red flags started waving immediately. First of all, the coworker of my friend wasn't in church ... any church. Secondly, he was over ten years older than me! If that wasn't enough to send me packing, the fact that he had a daughter with his previous girlfriend should have done the trick! I had barely turned twenty, but I thought I was old enough to handle a thirty-year-old.

The night went all right. He took me to a fun restaurant in Royal Oak, and we were not short on conversation. But I didn't feel comfortable. He kept rubbing my arm, squeezing my shoulder, and leaning over to whisper in my ear. I tried to make it clear from the beginning that I was a Christian (to which, he only laughed) and tried to keep my distance, but this guy wasn't taking the hint.

As he paid the bill (and I had requested paying for my half), he winked and said, "Let's continue this at my place."

I was floored! Sure I was a naïve, Christian, twenty-year old girl, but I knew exactly what he implied. As we walked to his car, I wanted to kick myself for having him pick me up.

When he opened the door for us to leave, I decided to clarify things right there. "I'll need to be going home," I said.

He tried to convince me it was only to watch movies. Eventually he said, "You know what? You're the kind of good girl I need in my life."

Maybe I had misjudged this guy! He took me home, told me he had a nice time, and said he'd call me. Even though I spent the majority of the date uncomfortable, my opinion had completely changed, and I hoped he would call me!

When I hadn't heard from him in over a week, I succumbed to the pressure and asked my friend to see what was up. My friend immediately looked guilty.

"What?" I asked.

"I don't know how to say this...."

My stomach fell. I knew this wasn't going to be good. "Just tell me."

"He said ... you weren't his type."

"What's his type?"

"I don't want to tell you."

My friend eventually did tell me. I guess his coworker said that I was uptight and a little fat. And it didn't matter that I hadn't been sold on the guy to begin with. Those words hurt. A lot. Any confidence I had before the date got taken down a few notches.

\* \* \*

Why does rejection from strangers hurt? We don't even know them! Yet, if you're like me, I've cried way too many times from strangers' comments.

Rejection leaves a deep wound no matter what, whether a spouse leaves or treats us in a way where we don't feel loved (as discussed last chapter) or when a guy insults you because he knows it'll hurt. Relationships with the opposite sex can be complicated, and we women seem to care what the guys think.

- Has your significant other ever critiqued something you were wearing?
- Has he ever—God forbid—mentioned something about your weight?
- Has he given an off-handed compliment about another woman that had you on edge?

Why do these things bother us? Because it is important for us women to feel special, to feel beautiful, and to feel appreciated (and let me add, it's important for our men to feel that way, too). When a stranger or some guy we barely know criticizes us, it can sometimes feel worse. At least with a significant other we can rationalize that he loves us and is trying to help. A stranger has completely different motives.

Several years ago, I attended a University of Michigan game and needed to leave the stadium. A young man stood by the gate leading out of the stadium. I had to ask a question about leaving and entering. Since he had on a uniform, I thought he would assist me. Instead when I went to approach him, he curled his lip and looked the other way. "I have a quick question," I said as politely as possible, already feeling insecure by his nonverbal actions. He did respond with a one-word answer, but as I walked away, he yelled, "And don't ever talk to me again, you fat [expletive]."

I might have had no idea who that guy was, but do you think his words hurt? Do you think I felt rejected? I did. I was a happily married woman with a child who adored me, yet I could barely get through the rest of the game because I was so crushed.

Ladies, here's the thing: we put way too much emphasis on how these men view us, and not nearly enough importance on how God sees us.

> *Here is the most important question: how does God see you?*

Easier said than done, right?

And that's only the opinion of strangers! What about when you're dating or looking for a serious relationship? Over half of adult women are currently unmarried, and the percentage increases for young women under the age of thirty-five.* For men, approximately 70 percent are unmarried under the age of thirty-five.* These statistics are wreaking havoc on relationships and cultural standards, leaving many women without a groom. For many women not married, trying to find any gentlemen who will actually treat them like a lady becomes an almost impossible task.

Because of this, women struggle with feelings of rejection when men deny them the commitment and longevity of a relationship that they long for most. The superficial takes center stage, and women can sometimes feel as if they are losing their identities and sense of self-worth in an effort to secure a man's attention.

Let's be real: today's culture is shifting. Last chapter might have studied how to overcome rejection from a spouse's lack of love, but more and more, adults do not want to even make the commitment of marriage. This unwillingness to commit only creates more rejection in an already critical world.

When did it become the "in" thing to not commit?

> *A major reason for a lack of commitment is that we, as a society, have turned away from Godly principles. This, in turn, negatively impacts our relationships.*

Our cultural climate is not helping to establish Godly relationships, and women are just as much to blame as the men. Many single women are not saving themselves for marriage and are having children outside of wedlock. That might seem like outdated thinking, but it has caused detrimental ramifications.

- In today's culture, saving sex for marriage is the exception, not the rule.
- Women are more forward with initiating sexual activity with men while dating.
- Over half of the children born today are born outside of wedlock.
- Fathers and husbands are seen as bumbling idiots on TV and in movies.
- Many women have taken away the "chase," and instead "chase" the men.
- The definition of family has been blurred.
- Men see that the commitment of marriage is not needed to be intimate and to have a family.

Unfortunately, these statistics make dissolving the relationship that much easier. Cohabitating couples who are not married are more than twice as likely to end their relationship than couples who are married.* All of these examples lead to a generation of women who are working more and raising children, but oftentimes by themselves. Young adult men up until their thirties might see it as liberating. Why be responsible and marry and do the right thing when they get their desires met without having to give of themselves in an emotionally intimate, respectable relationship?

Some may say that we women do this to ourselves, that we have created this cultural climate—thanks to feminism and the sexual revolution—that has made men question themselves and their own roles in our lives. And there is definitely blame to go around. However, that doesn't make rejection go away in our current situation. It doesn't make the single woman feel any better about another ended relationship because the man wasn't ready to commit.

## Tamar

> *And Judah took a wife for Er his firstborn, whose name was Tamar. And Er, Judah's firstborn, was wicked in the sight of the* LORD*; and the* LORD *slew him. And Judah said unto Onan, Go in unto thy brother's wife, and marry her, and raise up seed to thy brother. And Onan knew that the seed should not be his; and it came to pass, when he went in unto his brother's wife, that he spilled it on the ground, lest that he should give seed to his brother. And the thing which he did displeased the* LORD*: wherefore he slew him also. Then said Judah to Tamar his daughter in law, Remain a widow at thy father's house, till Shelah my son be grown: for he said, Lest peradventure he die also, as his brethren did. And Tamar went and dwelt in her father's house. And in process of time the daughter of Shuah Judah's wife died; and Judah was comforted, and went up unto his sheepshearers to Timnath, he and his friend Hirah the Adullamite. And it was told Tamar, saying, Behold thy father in law goeth up to Timnath to shear his sheep. And she put her widow's garments off from her, and covered her with a vail, and wrapped herself, and sat in an open place, which is by the way to Timnath; for she saw that Shelah was grown, and she was not given unto him to wife.*
>
> *Genesis 38*

Nobody wanted Tamar. She was the daughter-in-law of Judah (the same Judah, son of Leah) married to Judah's firstborn who died because he was up to no good. Jewish custom decreed that the dead husband's brother would marry the widow, in order for her to have a child. Tamar, based on evidence from Scripture, wanted to be able to conceive. Unfortunately, Onan didn't want

Tamar and set it up so that she would not have a child by him. If that wasn't bad enough, Judah promised Tamar that the youngest brother could be hers when he became of age, yet Judah had lied. When Shelah had grown they did not marry, and she was all but swept under the rug.

Tamar got pushed aside enough that she became desperate. The longer Judah ignored Tamar, the less likely she would ever be a fulfilled woman with children of her own. What do we women do when we become desperate? We take matters in our own hands. Which is exactly what Tamar did. Genesis 38 continues that she took off her widow's clothes and dressed as a harlot, covering her face, so no one could see who she was. Tamar tricked Judah, her own father-in-law, to lay with her:

> *When Judah saw her, he thought her to be an harlot; because she had covered her face. And he turned unto her by the way, and said, Go to, I pray thee, let me come in unto thee; (for he knew not that she was his daughter in law.) And she said, What wilt thou give me, that thou mayest come in unto me? And he … came in unto her, and she conceived by him. And she arose, and went away, and laid by her vail from her, and put on the garments of her widowhood …*

Even though Tamar might have conceived and given birth to twins, not even Judah wanted anything more to do with her. He never touched her after that. Had Tamar hoped that Judah would marry her after he found out she was pregnant with his children (she had twins)? She must have because having children outside of marriage was more than frowned upon, it was a killing offense. Sure, Judah spared her life when he realized he was the father, but he didn't want anything to do with her after that exchange.

Do you think she wondered, *What's wrong with me?* I do.

Tamar probably struggled with insecurities and heartache just like us. Did she try to entrap Judah not only to bear her own children, but also to secure his hand in marriage? By trying to manipulate the situation, she might have become pregnant, but she spent the rest of her life with the stigma of being rejected by men.

Just like us, Tamar must have felt the sting of rejection.

### *Final Thoughts*

Tamar might have made some poor decisions, but God still proved faithful to her. He saw her isolation and her rejection. Not only did she give birth to twins, but one of her sons, Perez, is ancestor to the House of David, and ultimately to Jesus Christ. God took her questionable circumstances and still brought His ultimate purpose and plan through her.

So, don't give up!

Being single and desiring companionship has never been easy, and today's world makes it even more challenging. Add your Christianity to the mix and you might already want to throw in the towel. Why put your heart out there when rejection is inevitable, right?

Wrong!

We might not be able to alter the changing tide of our cultural climate, but we can start with ourselves.

> *Search me, O God, and know my heart: try*
> *me, and know my thoughts.*
> Psalm 139:23

- Put God first. Don't let the opinions of men come before your relationship with Jesus.

- See yourself as God sees you. How can you expect others to see your value when you don't see it in yourself?
- Do not compromise who you are in Christ. If you have to be disobedient to the Word, then you are outside the will of God. God's umbrella of protection does not keep you when you step outside of His will.
- Remember, God has a purpose for your life. Don't try to take over. Trust that God knows what He's doing.

> *For I know the thoughts that I think toward you,*
> *saith the LORD, thoughts of peace, and not of evil,*
> *to give you an expected end.*
> *Jeremiah 29:11*

# CHAPTER SIX

## *Rejected by Her Father Michal*

The first man in a girl's life is her father, or so it should be.

Not every girl has a father in her life, so I'm grateful for mine. He may have been stricter than most, but I never questioned where I stood with him.

My dad was a blue-collar union worker at GM, waking up at 5:00 AM and working overtime as much as he could. He never went to college, joining the army as a young man and getting married not long after that. He and my mom walked into one of those crazy churches in the seventies, becoming tongue-talking Pentecostals, much to the chagrin of his Catholic parents and her Baptist ones.

The greatest thing my father ever did for me and my siblings—and I can admit it now, even though as a child, I might have thought differently—was take us to church. We lived and breathed church. Church on Sundays, Wednesdays, or any other days of revivals and prayer meetings. Basically, church was not optional.

Sick? Go to church and get prayed for.

Sleepover on a Saturday night? Not unless the friend was taking you to church.

School activities? Not if they fell on Wednesdays or any other day there was a church function.

I looked up to my dad. He was charismatic and confident. He had friends everywhere, from his bowling league to fellow deer hunters to church guys. If something needed done, he'd get it done. He also never accepted excuses. All four of his children knew that when he said no, it was no. There was no whining, no pleading, and definitely no complaining. Anything thought of as rebellious would be handled swiftly. And he expected the same hard work from us kids.

That's why my parents' divorce rocked my world.

Why did my dad give up? He never gave up.

Why didn't he try to make it work?

Questions exploded inside me. I wanted it to make sense, but it didn't. Church felt weird. Dad wasn't there. What would people say? Couples didn't get divorced at my church. At least, in my nineteen-year-old mind, that's what I told myself. Now we would have to face everyone.

After my parents split, I refused contact with my father for months. A part of me was angry that he dissolved the marriage and our family unit, another part of me was confused because my mother was so distraught. I didn't think she could handle me seeing my dad. But mostly I saw it as rejection.

Those few months were some of the hardest of my life. I had been very fortunate up until that point to have a strong relationship with my father. He could be stern, but he would also do anything for us kids if it was within his reach. Dad had tried to contact me, even tried calling me while I worked. Giving him the cold shoulder became exhausting. Here I had a father who wanted a relationship with me, who desired to reconcile, and I could only build a wall between us.

In this case, I was treating my father exactly how I wouldn't want him to treat me. My wrong actions were spurred on by the rejection I felt through the whole ordeal. I felt my mother's pain, and I transferred it onto myself and my relationship with my father.

Thankfully, my father didn't give up on me. He gave me space, but he would keep sending reminders that he wanted to talk, that he loved me, that he was sorry for how things unfolded with Mom. I firmly believe I would not have achieved as much as I did in my life if it wasn't for the steady hand of my dad, keeping me on the straight and narrow.

I realize my story might not even touch the surface of the pain and rejection you feel or have felt toward your relationship—or lack of one—with your father. This specific relationship is one of the most important for children and teens. When a father is out of the picture—whatever the reason may be—a vital piece to the nuclear family is taken out of the equation.

This doesn't mean that those who had little to no relationship with their father can't grow up to be successful, happy people. However, there is more dysfunction in the family unit than ever before, and it affects how children behave and how they view themselves. Plenty of research comes to the same conclusion: kids need their father and do better with him in their lives. Teens do especially well when the father has a daily connection and relationship with them. *

The father-daughter relationship shapes the girl's life and how she views and behaves around men.* Therefore, if a father hurts his daughter—whether physically, mentally, verbally, emotionally— the wound has the potential to shape and define her negatively.

How would you describe your relationship with your father? Answer the following questions to get a better idea of the influence he has had on you:

1. Have you ever felt rejected by your father? Describe this.

   _____

   _____

2. Did your father have a good relationship with your mother?

   _____

   _____

3. How did your father handle conflict?

   _____

   _____

4. What fond memories do you have of your father? What feelings describe how you felt during those times?

   _____

   _____

5. What three words would you use to describe your father's temperament?

   _____

   _____

6. Would you want your husband (or future husband) to act toward you the way your father acted toward your mother? Why?

   _____

   _____

Please understand that many of you reading this may have had wonderful relationships with your fathers—and still do. That's the way it should be! However, sometimes even those of us with strong relationships with our fathers have struggled with rejection in some way—whether intentional or not—from our fathers' words or actions. Then, there are those of you who have no relationship with your father. Maybe you've never met him, or maybe he walked out when you were young. Maybe there are abuse issues that you have no desire to relive. There are others who have a strained relationship.

In order to get to the root of our rejection, so that we may overcome it, we have to be honest with ourselves about where our initial feelings of rejection came from.

### *Michal*

> *And Michal Saul's daughter loved David: and they told Saul, and the thing pleased him. And Saul said, I will give him her, that she may be a snare to him, and that the hand of the Philistines may be against him.*
> *I Samuel 18:21*

Michal had a lot of things going for her. She was born a princess to one of the greatest monarchs of the Hebrew nation. Not only did she have royal blood, but she was also a famed beauty. She may have lived in a palace, but her life was far from perfect. According to Biblical tradition, King Saul had too many battles to fight and a kingdom and concubine to keep. His interactions with either of his daughters were rare. The princess barely saw him.

The few interactions we see in the Bible between father and daughter are when Michal is already a young woman. The Bible doesn't show the king thinking warmly of his daughter or spending quality time with her. Back then, daughters were considered property and used as a way to gain more land or acquire more wealth or to merge two kingdoms together.

But Michal was already in love.

She had already set her sights on the handsome shepherd and lyre player, David of Bethlehem. This, however, wouldn't be a suitable union. Her father would never allow a shepherd to marry a princess.

Then David killed Goliath, became a hero, and things changed. We might think that it would work out well for Michal. After all, the king had promised that whoever killed Goliath could marry one of his daughters. Not exactly warm and mushy, but in this case the giant-slayer happened to be the one who held Michal's heart. Too bad that Saul decided Merab, the older sister, should marry David.

To make matters worse, King Saul had a problem with Israel's new hero, David. After David killed Goliath, he became unstoppable. Anything the king threw at him, David handled with wisdom and humility. The king had become incredibly jealous. No one should receive accolades other than the king. Saul needed to trap David. Basically, he wanted him dead.

What better way to lure David to his death than to use the princess? When King Saul found out that Michal loved David, he did the unthinkable: he used his daughter as a manipulative tool to trap and kill the young man who was stealing all of his glory. Merab, the first daughter, got pawned off on someone else, and Michal received the news she'd been hoping for. Only, the king wasn't expecting a marriage. He assumed David would be dead before then.

The king's plan was simple. In order for David to marry Michal, he must accomplish the impossible. Saul tasked him with the assignment of 100 Philistine foreskins. That meant killing and mutilating 100 of Israel's enemies. Sounds gross and unlikely, right?

Saul didn't expect David to live through that! Sorry, Michal, your dad just used you to lure David to his death.

When David surprised the king by coming back from the mission *very alive* and with double amount of proof needed that his task had been successful, King Saul had no choice but to give his daughter to David.

If the story stopped here, there might have been hope for the lovely Michal. Sure her father used her as bait, but the king's plan was not successful, and she got to marry the young man she loved.

Unfortunately, Saul wasn't finished. He became even more determined to kill David, even at the expense of his daughter. Motivated to kill David who was now on the run, King Saul forced Michal to marry another man—against her wishes.

> But Saul had given Michal his daughter, David's wife,
> to Phalti the son of Laish, which was of Gallim.
> I Samuel 25:44

How do we know that Michal was upset over this forced decision? Because she loved David deeply, and they were still within their first year or two of marriage. She loved him still because she helped him escape King Saul even though she knew it would bring his wrath upon her. The Bible insinuates that she did not consummate the marriage to Phalti, and she bore him no children. This shows that she took her covenant with David seriously.

The real atrocity out of all of this is that King Saul hurt Michal so deeply. Some may argue that King Saul was hardly a good father, but how did he reject his daughter?

Simple. By rejecting his daughter's feelings. By rejecting her value as a human being. By rejecting her marriage covenant with David.

This story doesn't end well. Michal became bitter. When David came back to take his wife who had been stolen from him, the situation had changed. He now had other wives. Michal was not the one and only. King Saul might not have killed David, but by ripping apart the newlyweds like he did, he dissolved his daughter's hope.

## Final Thoughts

Sometimes life does not happen the way we planned. We have it all mapped out from a young age. First, we fall in love, then we get married, then we have happy children (one girl and one boy). We don't expect that our marriage will be in shambles, or that we find out we're pregnant from a man who has no interest in a committed relationship. What then?

For many of us, we have struggled almost our entire lives with rejection because the one man who was supposed to love us and be there for us … wasn't.

A girl needs her father. In our imperfect world, many children grow up without a strong father-figure. This can raise questions:

- Why didn't my dad stay?
- Did he stop loving me? Has he *ever* loved me?
- Did I do something wrong?

A father's rejection, no matter the circumstances, can lead to mistrust in men, to broken relationships, to skewed self-image. Just like Michal, bitterness can take hold.

But *we do* have a father who cares. *We do* have a father who loves us and sees the best in us. *We do* have a father who protects us and keeps us safe.

> *Or what man is there of you, whom if his son*
> *[daughter] ask for bread, will he give him [her] a*
> *stone? Or if he [she] ask a fish, will he give him [her]*
> *a serpent? If ye then, being evil, know how to give*
> *good gifts unto your children, how much more shall*
> *your Father which is in heaven give good things to*
> *them that ask him?*
> *Matthew 7:9-11*

Sometimes it is hard to imagine the goodness and generosity of our Heavenly Father. This is especially true if you are new to a relationship with Jesus Christ. All of us can fall into the trap of viewing God the way we view other people. So we become standoffish, not really believing everything the Bible says about our Heavenly Father:

- He loves me unconditionally?
  - o *Yeah, right.*
- He doesn't look on the outside, but He sees who I am on the inside?
  - o *Sure, whatever you say.*
- When He forgives, He forgets?
  - o *Are you kidding? No one ever forgets.*
- He will take care of my needs?
  - o *Tell that to my bills!*
- He wants me to live a joyful, peaceful, and content life?
  - o *Well, that's not going to happen!*

Why do we have such a hard time believing that the sovereign God of the universe knows who we are as individuals (even knows the number of hairs upon our head) and cares for us more than any human being could?

> *Behold the fowls of the air: for they sow not,*
> *neither do they reap, nor gather into barns; yet*
> *your heavenly Father feedeth them. Are ye not*
> *much better than they?*
> *Matthew 6:26*

Could it be that we have a hard time letting go of the rejection that we have experienced? Maybe it's hard to see God as a loving father because you struggled your entire life without an earthly one.

It's time you tried. Don't let the hurt over your father's actions or his absence from your life turn you bitter. Michal's story from the Bible is one of caution. She might have been a princess, but she suffered one rejection after another because of the self-serving decisions of her father. Instead of overcoming it and turning to God, she dabbled in idolatry and turned cynical and calloused as an older woman.

God has better plans for you than you could ever fathom. Let Him love you and take care of you and comfort you. Let your rejection go, and let God fill your void.

> *Behold, what manner of love the Father hath*
> *bestowed upon us, that we should be called the*
> *sons [and daughters] of God...*
> *I John 3:1*

# CHAPTER SEVEN

## *Rejected by Other Women*
## *Woman at the Well*

My session with the Bible College president and board had just ended. Mom told me to go to my dorm and pack up the rest of my things. We had a long drive from Delaware back to Michigan, and Mom wanted to leave as soon as possible. And I did, too.

I walked into the dorms, still littered with a handful of students needing to take their finals. I hoped none of them knew about what happened. I was already broken enough. Hopefully, my girlfriends could pick up my spirits.

As I passed the girls in the hall, none made eye contact.

I swallowed back the hurt.

These had been my friends. We had laughed together, taken classes together, talked about boys together, and even prayed together. My actions at the college had been very wrong, make no mistake about it, but I knew the secrets of all of these girls. I knew the rules they had broken, too. The only difference between us is that I had gotten caught.

As I packed in my almost empty dorm room, I kept wondering why the girls were acting like they were. It didn't make sense. We were *friends*. At that moment, I heard one of my close buddies in the hall laughing with someone. Needing some understanding and camaraderie, I went out to the hall and said, "Hi, Lynn."

She looked over at me, and her smile immediately disappeared. The other girl she had been talking to wouldn't even look at me. Instead she left us standing there without another word.

Grasping at straws, I asked, "How're your finals going?"

Lynn didn't say anything at first. Minute by minute, my heart broke a little more. Finally she blurted, "Why are you talking to me?"

"Because … we're friends…." My heart kept breaking.

"No, we're not!" she snapped. "You're a liar, Janice. Everyone here knows it. We know what you did. And I, for one, can't be friends with someone like you."

I stood in the hall, my heart shattered at my feet while she stormed past me to her dorm.

* * *

I wish I could say that after my painful experience with Lynn at the Bible College I never felt rejected by other women, especially my friends, again. But I can't say that. Sometimes it would be little things, such as ladies all going out to lunch together and me not being invited, but those I learned to brush off. I was no longer going to be that little girl rejected because she wasn't invited to a birthday party.

There have been times, however, when I have been rejected by women I loved and cherished, such as my childhood best friend.

That situation hurt me so deeply because I loved her like a sister. We went camping together, and to amusement parks, church camps, and nearly every weekend one of us had crashed at the other's house. She listened to me cry when I got busted at Bible College, and I listened to her cry over a boyfriend's breakup. We were involved in each other's weddings and began to hang out on double dates with our husbands.

Until one day when it just stopped. She stopped calling. She stopped talking to me at church. She would completely ignore me, even if I would directly say hello to her.

There had to be reasons, right? I've thought the same thing. Somehow I must have done something wrong. Maybe I hurt her. Unintentional hurt is still hurt. Maybe I said something or behaved in a way where *she* felt hurt or rejected. But should someone still hold a grudge when one apologizes? I vividly remember standing outside of a ladies' banquet begging her to forgive me. I wasn't even sure I understood what I did wrong, but she was my *best friend*. I would beg if I had to. Unfortunately, it wasn't enough. She had decided that our close friendship was over.

It hurts me even to write it, but I'm not one who lets toxic feelings hang around. If someone is upset, I want to fix it. If I can't fix it, I pray about it. Only God can heal the hidden hurts that even best friends can't see.

Being rejected by men is one thing, but sometimes being rejected by women hurts all the more. Women are sometimes brutal to each other. Not with fists, but with words. We are our worst critics, and women's judgment on each other makes life sometimes feel like a competition.

Women can be:

- Cliquish
- Jealous
- Intimidated

- Petty
- Gossips
- Self-righteous
- Critical and Fault-Finding

I know I can be guilty of these things as well. We women are the first to notice if someone has lost or gained weight, if someone's relationship has tanked, if someone's fashion sense needs work. If another woman's life is actually going well—maybe she has focused on her health and it's showing, or she is going to get married to a wonderful man, or she seems to get everything she wants—it can be difficult for some of us to simply be happy for her.

This competitive nature of women has been around for as long as we have. Do we realize the effect we have on our fellow women when we resort to treating each other with hostility, envy, and pettiness? Trust me, a woman may look like she's put together and she has it all going for her, but no one is immune to meanness or judgment.

### The Woman at the Well

*And [Jesus] must needs go through Samaria ...*

*Now Jacob's well was there. Jesus therefore, being wearied with his journey, sat thus on the well: and it was about the sixth hour.*

*There cometh a woman of Samaria to draw water:*

*Jesus saith unto her, Give me to drink ...*

*Then saith the woman of Samaria unto him, How is it that thou, being a Jew, askest drink of me, which am a woman of Samaria?*

*for the Jews have no dealings with the Samaritans.*

*Jesus answered and said unto her, If thou knewest the gift of God,*

> *and who it is that saith to thee, Give me to drink;*
>
> *thou wouldest have asked of him,*
>
> *and he would have given thee living water …*
>
> *Whosoever drinketh of this water shall thirst again: But whosoever*
>
> *drinketh of the water that I shall give him shall never thirst; but the*
>
> *water that I shall give him shall be in him*
>
> *a well of water springing up into everlasting life.*
>
> *The woman saith unto him,*
>
> *Sir, give me this water, that I thirst not, neither come hither to draw.*
>
> *Jesus saith unto her, Go, call thy husband, and come hither.*
>
> *The woman answered and said, I have no husband.*
>
> *Jesus said unto her, Thou hast well said, I have no husband:*
>
> *For thou hast had five husbands;*
>
> *and he whom thou now hast is not thy husband:*
>
> *in that saidst thou truly.*
>
> *The woman saith unto him, Sir, I perceive that thou art a prophet …*
>
> *John 4:4–19*

Two important pieces of information about the woman at the well. First, she was a Samaritan. This is why she is surprised Jesus is speaking to her. Jews did not associate with Samaritans. They considered Samaritans beneath them because they had Gentile blood in them. The second important piece of information is that not only was she a Samaritan, she was living in sin. The man she was with was not her husband. If having five husbands wasn't enough to make the town of Samaria talk, living in sin with a man would definitely make her an outcast.

The woman was so much an outcast that she had to come to the well when all the other women had left. In Biblical times, women gathered at the well to socialize. Think of it as a social club. The woman at the well was so much on the outside of the women's circle that she had to draw water in the middle of the day when the other women weren't present. She came when no one was there, leading the reader to believe that she was unwelcomed and unwanted.

Was she bitter? The first words out of her mouth to Jesus basically asked, "Why are you talking to me?"

How rejected she must have felt living all of her days ostracized by the women in her community. Even when she ran back to the village to share her meeting with Jesus, the Bible specifically states that she went to *the men*:

> *The woman then left her waterpot,*
> *and went her way into the city, and saith to the men,*
> *Come, see a man, which told me*
> *all things that ever I did:*
> *is not this the Christ? Then they went out of the city,*
> *and came unto him.*
> *John 4:28–30*

The fact that she felt more comfortable going to the men shows the disconnect she had with the women of the town.

Why is that?

This woman would have been considered dirty, ungodly, and a harlot. She would have not only been shunned by the women, but they would have told their children not to talk to her and would have cast judgmental glances her way. She had to keep to herself, isolated and abandoned by all, except for the man who did not value her enough to marry her.

But meeting Jesus changed her. Jesus saw her value and waited at the well specifically for *her*. And He didn't need the other women's opinions to start the revival in Samaria. He chose the one lone woman at the well. He chose *her*. He went out of the way because He saw her potential despite her flaws.

### Final Thoughts

Acceptance among our peers drives many of us to look and act certain ways. From fashion to food to the way we carry ourselves to even the way we raise our children, something within us longs for acceptance and friendship, especially among other women. Invariably, we join our groups, start our circles, and seek out those who fit well within what and who we are. The old slogan, "Birds of a feather flock together," rings a certain truth.

First, we must be careful that we don't become like the women of the well who excluded the one.

- Kindness goes a long way.
- See other women as Jesus sees them.
- Don't judge. Many times we don't know the whole story.
- Instead of gossiping, pray for each other.
- Leave criticism at the door. None of us are perfect.
- Love. Always, always love.

If you are the woman who feels rejected by so-called friends or other women in general, recognize it for what it is and move on. One of my dear friends once told me, "You can't control what other people say or do, you can only control what *you* say and do."

The woman at the well testified that day, spreading the gospel and introducing Jesus to her community. Because of her, many of the Samaritans believed on Jesus:

> *And many of the Samaritans of that city believed on him for the saying of the woman, which testified, He told me all that ever I did. So when the Samaritans were come unto him, they besought him that he would tarry with them: and he abode there two days. And many more believed because of his own word; And said unto the woman, Now we believe, not because of thy saying: for we have heard him ourselves, and know that this is indeed the Christ, the Savior of the world.*

When Philip arrived in Samaria in Acts chapter 8—after Jesus had already ascended unto heaven—and began to preach to the Samaritans, revival occurred. Peter and John actually came to help Philip because the revival was so great. Could it be that the woman at the well put into motion God's plan for saving outcasts, such as the Samaritans? And that He used an outcast among the outcasts to do that?

Being rejected by other women may be ostracizing and isolating, but remember: God sees in you what others cannot see.

> *For the LORD seeth not as man [woman] seeth; for man [woman] looketh on the outward appearance, but the LORD looketh on the heart.*
> *I Samuel 16:7*

So, don't fret about the style of your clothes, whether or not you're wearing name brands, what size you're wearing, or if you're hairstyle fits the newest trend.

Be the kind of woman you want to encounter. Recognize that God created you for a reason. You have a purpose in Him that is not reliant on the pettiness and opinions of other women.

Do you have a past? God still has a purpose for you.

Do you live with regrets? God still has a purpose for you.

Do you feel as if you will never be able to "fit in?" God still has a purpose for you.

# CHAPTER EIGHT

## *Rejected by Coworkers*
## *Hagar*

I walked into the middle school's principal's office curious as to why he called me in. My second year of teaching seventh grade reading and literacy classes was off to a strong start. It might have taken me a little while during the first year to acclimate to the middle school setting, especially after three years at the high school, but I had finally found my footing and felt reasonably sure that I was doing the job to the best of my ability.

"Sit down," he said.

As I sat, I noticed the dean of the middle school students also sitting in the office, and he seemed to be looking anywhere but at me.

The principal took a yellow legal pad and started flipping through the paper. "The other reading teachers have been coming to me with some complaints. About you."

To say I was shocked would be an understatement. The three other women who taught the reading classes (two teaching it in the eighth grade and one teaching it with me in the seventh grade) had been nothing but kind to me when I first came over from the high school. They had all taught at the middle school for years; I was the newcomer, but they seemed to be nice. We met up a few times at one of their homes, we prepped together, we went to conferences together. In complete transparency, I thought the three women had become my friends. So, to have the principal start reading from his notes of all of things the other teachers did not like about me was like taking a knife and stabbing me in the back … repeatedly.

The accusations were almost entirely without merit:

I was accused of not teaching. This was the biggest one. They were concerned that students were not receiving the entire curriculum. Supposedly, I just sat at my desk and let my students read the whole hour. This accusation bothered me the most because I took pride in my teaching ability and creativity. I thoroughly enjoyed the lessons that were created with the team and taught to the students.

Another accusation that cut deep alleged me of not being a team player. Supposedly, I did my own thing and I didn't like working with the group.

I was accused of leaving a conference early.

Another complaint was that I wasn't taking the job seriously.

The third teacher, the one who worked with me with the seventh grade students, complained that I would not let her discipline my students.

In all fairness I am far from perfect, and everyone, including myself, needs to grow and improve. I have never been so stubborn or arrogant to believe I was above constructive criticism. But sitting in the middle school principal's office, I felt completely blindsided.

The tears came. It embarrassed me to cry in front of this principal who stared at me stone-faced, but when I feel attacked, that's my natural response. Thinking about it now, I wish I would have been strong enough in who I was as a person and who I was in Christ to stand up for myself. But I had been too floored at the truth. The three women, instead of going to me so we could work it out as professionals and friends, all went above my head to put me in my place.

The principal and I had a mutual respectful working relationship before this incident. Because of the three women's effort in calling me and my supposed errors out, the principal ended the session with: "Don't think you can come from the high school and do things your own way. From now on I will be watching you."

Pushing past the stress and high anxiety of working in hostile conditions, I threw myself into helping the students. I volunteered my summers for a reading program that was highly successful among the middle school students, I tutored students at the local library, student literacy scores continued to show vast improvement every year, and when students expressed interest in putting on a play, I volunteered after school for there to be a drama club, where students could put on a theatrical production. Those examples were highlights of some tough years in my career. On one hand, I was publicly honored by a board member in the district for excellence in education for my work with the middle school students, yet on the other hand, I'd have to sit in meetings with the principal and the three other teachers and listen to them vent about how I wasn't doing what they wanted, when they wanted, etc.

It got to be so stressful my skin condition became increasingly worse. My husband and I, who had tried for years to have a second child, found out we were expecting. Three days after one of the previously mentioned "vent" sessions, I lost my unborn child, at twenty weeks gestation, and had to deliver him in the emergency room. Working at the middle school for a total of five years nearly pushed me over the edge. They were the worst in my professional career. It was like I had a target on my back. I could do no right. No matter how hard I tried doing exactly what they wanted me to do, it was never enough. They simply didn't like me, and they didn't want me there.

My husband one day said the magic words, "Janice, just quit. You are better than this." And after years of praying for a way out, I got word from a friend that the high school had another English vacancy. I requested a transfer. The middle school principal didn't thank me for any of my successful work at the middle school. He simply said, "Yes, that's probably a good idea that you go back."

So, I did. Broken, bruised, and bullied.

* * *

Nearly 75 percent of us women work outside the home.* That makes us busy and under pressure. Add to the fact that there are more girls enrolled in colleges than their male counterparts, and we women now have to deal with a myriad of work– or school-related conversations and relationships than even ten or twenty years ago.* Our culture continues to change in terms of women's roles both inside and outside the home. Whether it's by choice or necessity, women are working and outside the four walls of their family unit.

Books have been written about work-related conflict and how to get along with these individuals you spend forty or more hours a week with, not to mention all the personality tests that highlight the strengths and weaknesses of your personality and that of others. These books and tests serve a purpose, but sometimes conflicts arise despite the self-help books. Sometimes coworkers are spiteful, or cliquish, or abrasive in their quest for promotion.

Many times our managers can be oppressive or hard-hearted, making the work day unbearable. Over 70 percent of the American labor force do not like their jobs, and over 60 percent of workers in another survey admitted that their bosses hurt their self-esteem.*

That's a lot of unhappiness going around. Could the culprit be rejection?

- Do you feel left out or excluded at work?
- Do you feel your boss favors others unfairly?
- Does your boss act like a dictator, making you second-guess yourself and walk on egg shells?
- Do you work with someone who criticizes you, especially in front of others?
- Do you work with someone who tries to "one-up" you, or take the credit for work you've done?
- Has someone else received a promotion you feel should have been yours?

If you answered yes to any of these questions, then you have most likely felt rejected at work in some form. Some of you might experience the type of toxic work environment I had to endure at the middle school. This type of constant stress and rejection — whether for something as simple as not fitting in to something as serious as being berated regularly — can wear on a woman's soul.

I know because I endured it.

As I look back, the only way I survived the emotional turmoil I had to walk through on a daily basis was the Lord. He became my rock like never before. I would bring my desperate tears, my anxiety, my anger, and I would leave it at his feet. And I prayed that He would deliver me. I prayed that He would take me out of the situation.

Thankfully, He did.

## *Hagar*

> *And Sarai said unto Abram, Behold now, the LORD hath restrained me from bearing: I pray thee, go in unto my maid; it may be that I may obtain children by her. And Abram hearkened to the voice of Sarai … And he went in unto Hagar, and she conceived: and when she saw that she had conceived, her mistress was despised in her eyes. And Sarai said unto Abram, My wrong be upon thee: I have given my maid into thy bosom; and when she saw that she had conceived, I was despised in her eyes: the LORD judge between me and thee. But Abram said unto Sarai, Behold, thy maid is in thine hand; do to her as it pleaseth thee. And when Sarai dealt hardly with her, she fled from her face. And the angel of the LORD found her by a fountain of water in the wilderness, by the fountain in the way to Shur. And he said, Hagar, Sarai's maid, whence camest thou? and whither wilt thou go? And she said, I flee from the face of my mistress Sarai. And the angel of the LORD said unto her, Return to thy mistress, and submit thyself under her hands … And the angel of the LORD said unto her, Behold, thou art with child and shalt bear a son, and shalt call his name Ishmael; because the LORD hath heard thy affliction.*
> *Genesis 16: 2–11*

Both Sarah and Hagar lived hard lives, and both were not perfect. Sarah, still called Sarai, became impatient and decided to take matters into her own hands. Unfortunately, Hagar paid the price. I realize Sarah was Abraham's wife, but the Bible shows a dark side to her.

Hagar, an Egyptian, was given to Abraham and Sarah while they were in Egypt. Consider how it felt for Hagar to leave the comforts of Egypt—a city well established beyond the times—as well as family and friends. Whether she was a servant of the pharaoh's, or a concubine, or something else altogether, traveling with a Hebrew tribe through the desert was probably not on her wish fulfillment list.

The Bible makes no indication that there was a problem between the two women until Sarah's reckless decision to speed up the waiting process with God. She gave Hagar to Abraham to be his wife. There is no record of Sarah clearing this idea with Hagar. On the contrary, Hagar, as a servant, had no say in the decision. When Hagar conceived, Sarah became overcome with jealousy. Why else would she have behaved so badly? Sarah must have realized what a mess she had created. Hagar was now a wife of Abraham and now carried his first heir. Hagar figured out she had what Sarah had yet to produce—an heir for Abraham—and the contention began.

The rejection Hagar endured in her work situation is staggering, especially when she had no say in the events. Sarah's insecurities caused a full-out attack on Hagar, dealing with her so harshly that Hagar ran away while pregnant. Whatever happened must have been intense enough that Hagar had to escape. The angel of the Lord stopped Hagar and told her to go back to Abraham because God was with her. That the child had a purpose and future.

It must have been hard for her to go back. Many of us have a difficult time staying in a job where our flesh doesn't want to be there, even though we know that's where God wants us. The same dilemma awaited Hagar. She probably had no desire to go back to the envious older woman who took her frustrations out on the Egyptian. Still, she had the promise of God that her child had a destiny. Because of that, Hagar stayed in an uncomfortable situation where she and her child could be taken care of.

The worst of the rejection, however, was when the promised child had been born of Sarah. Remember, God had already told Hagar that her child had a great destiny. Sarah didn't want the competition. She wanted her son, Isaac, to be the only heir of Abraham. So, what does she do? She fires Hagar. Even though Hagar was technically a wife of Abraham with his oldest heir, she forces Hagar and her son, Ishmael, to leave the tribe.

So now this newly single woman and her son are wandering the desert, trying to make it back to Egypt or anywhere they can establish a home. Dehydrated with no more water or food, Hagar sets her only son under a low-hanging bush and cries out to God.

Let me add that Sarah acted outside of the will of God. Twice.

First, she forced Abraham upon Hagar instead of waiting for her own promise. Then, she kicked Hagar and Ishmael out of the family. Remember, it was God's will for Hagar to be there. He sent an angel when she ran away the first time, telling her to go back because that's where she needed to be. By Sarah forcing her competition to pack up and leave, she was acting outside of God's plan.

Thankfully, God provided for Hagar and Ishmael. He saw their rejection and listened to their cries, supplying them with a well. Beyond that, He sustained them and blessed their lives. But how much of this would have never happened if Sarah had overcome her own insecurities and jealousy?

Hagar's rejection, for the most part, took place outside of her control. She was rejected for circumstances and events that were simply not her fault. And even after doing what she was told and conceiving and raising an heir for Abraham, she was fired and cast aside anyway.

### *Final Thoughts*

As I studied Hagar's story, I identified with her. I might not have ever been forced to marry and birth a child for a man and his wife, but I have had to work alongside vengeful, mean people. I have been blamed for situations completely outside of my control, and I have had fingers pointed at me for poor decisions others made.

If you have had to endure rejection at work, please know that you are not alone. Not only have many of us had to deal with similar situations at our jobs, but God is with every single one of us. We are never without Him. And He sees all. The book of Colossians in the New Testament reminds us that God sees everything:

> *But he that doeth wrong shall receive for the wrong which he hath done: and there is no respect of persons.*
> *Colossians 3:25*

When it comes to handling rejection—and breaking free from it—you have to give these situations to God. The more you dwell on unfairness or disrespect, the more it will eat at you and the more the root of rejection will grow inside you, leading to bitterness, anger, and insecurities. Do not give your coworkers or your boss that kind of leverage or power over you. Remind yourself of what Paul said in Romans:

> *And we know that **all things work together for good** to them that love God, to them who are the called according to his purpose.*
> *Romans 8:28*

God is working it out in our favor! And if you are in a desperate situation, like Hagar, God sees your anguish and hears your cries. He will answer you and direct your path.

# CHAPTER NINE

## *Rejected by Her Community*
## *Mary*

I sat on the church pew two rows from the front. The youth had the first three rows reserved for each service. Maybe it was to get us involved in the worship or maybe it was to keep an eye on us. Either way, every service my friends and I sat in the same spot. This service, however, I tried to sit anywhere but up front. I would have much rather sat in the back. Actually, I would have preferred not to have even come.

On this night, my mentor was going to have to go to the front of the church and publicly confess her sin. I looked up to Jennifer in so many ways. She had the best singing voice and was such a poised, beautiful young woman. Eight years older than me, she had taken me under her wing and had given me tips on hairstyles, clothes, and music. I was envious when she announced her engagement, but I was also thrilled for her. She would make a gorgeous bride.

A few of us knew about her pregnancy. Since she was already engaged and the marriage would be taking place in a few short weeks, I thought—and hoped—the scandal would blow over.

Because she led the youth and mentored several of us girls, many in the church community felt that she and Eric, her fiancé, needed to publicly acknowledge their sin and ask forgiveness. By doing so, it would help those of us who looked up to them to refrain from such behavior.

The whole service I thought I might puke. They actually had songs at the beginning, as if no one had any idea what was on the agenda. It was the white elephant in the room that everyone knew about.

When the pastor greeted the congregation and told us to sit down, I knew it was time. My heart felt heavy in my chest because deep down I knew this was wrong. As the couple made their way to the front, I felt embarrassed for them. I watched as Jennifer cried and apologized, then Eric. I wanted to jump up and hug her, to tell her that I felt her pain and embarrassment. But I didn't.

\* \* \*

In Shirley Jackson's short story, "The Lottery," the community gets together every year for a seemingly fun day of food and activities in the center of town. The twist of the story is that the get-together is for a lottery to determine who among the community will be sacrificed. Not exactly the happy ending expected for a story that starts off so upbeat. When writing this chapter, I remembered this story and how upsetting it was to me that the community would turn so fast on the poor woman whose name was drawn in the horrific lottery. The irony is that what happens in the story is the exact opposite of what community stands for.

What constitutes community? It's a group of people within proximity to each other that share a common goal, belief, or location. There is your local community where your residence is located, but you might also have a church community, a school community, a sport community, community within a career (such as army units), a social community, and lastly, a community within a hobby or skillset (such as Scrabble clubs and book clubs).

The whole idea of community is togetherness. Studies have shown that we have a need to belong or feel accepted within groups.* We actually need our communities for survival. We weren't meant for isolation.

When a group pulls away from an individual, feelings of rejection are likely to occur. Think of a football team. The linemen are supposed to protect the quarterback, so that the quarterback can be successful and complete the play. What happens when the opposing team occupies the linemen and one gets away? The quarterback is isolated and is most likely going to get sacked. Each position on that field is vitally important. Not only that, but each position has to work well with the team in order to make it down the field.

In a community, there is a sense of togetherness. Isolation does not take place when the community is strong and supportive.

When I was in fifth grade I had a group of friends. We were very close and would hang out every day at the playground. One of the girls was having a sleepover. The eight of us had a blast. I remember vividly the movies we watched, the pizza we ate, the songs we danced to, and the scary games we played. The next morning, I woke up to whispering. When I opened my eyes, the girls were all awake and were looking at me.

I asked what was happening, and one of the girls pointed at my sleeping bag. When I looked, I saw the carpet was wet underneath the sleeping bag. Even though I knew I hadn't peed my pants, it definitely looked like it!

No matter how much explaining I did, or the proof that my pajamas were in fact dry, those girls all looked at me with doubt on their faces. I remember how, in that moment, I felt extremely isolated. The sense of community had been broken by their suspicions.

On a greater scale, the same thing happened with my mentor, Jennifer. The sense of church community had been broken when church members decided she needed to be a lesson for us younger ladies. The public shaming must have been too much for the couple. Even though they were married at our church, they did not stay in our church for long after that. The days of her mentoring me were over.

The church community is arguably the most important community because the church is a fellowship of the believers. Yet many souls leave churches because of rejection, which leads to isolation. There has been a large exodus of people from churches in recent years. The reasons range from too much judgment to lacking in relevance, but I'd argue that people don't want to spend their Sunday mornings in a church where they feel rejected.

Questions to ask yourself:

- Have you forsaken church community because of judgmental attitudes?
- Have you forsaken church community because you don't feel you fit in?
- Have you forsaken church community because of your past? You don't feel good enough?
- Have you forsaken church community because it lacks relevance in your life? Have you asked yourself why you feel this way?
- We deal with enough rejection in the world, why deal with it on church on Sundays?

Let me encourage you! If you have struggled with rejection from your community (whatever community that might be), it is imperative to keep God the main thing in your life. He keeps everything in perspective. His strength is perfect, and He is ever faithful.

But what if you have had to deal with rejection from the *church* community? Just like I stated in the chapter on religious leaders, the church should be the refuge for all. It should not be a social club for the saints, but a hospital for the broken. If that's not what you've experienced, don't throw in the towel and walk away. Your soul is too important.

A few points to consider:

- Don't blame God for people's actions.
    o Just because a community is full of Christians doesn't mean they're all acting Christlike.
- God doesn't condemn, He convicts.
    o If you have done something wrong, don't get defensive. Repent and move on. God doesn't wallow in your sin, and neither should you. When He forgives you, it's gone.
    o Once you've asked God for forgiveness and you go to others to seek renewal, move on. Do not let people condemn you. I would even say to them, "God's forgiven me, so don't bring up my past anymore."
- Don't forsake the assembling of believers.
    o Find another church if you have to, but don't stop going! I know you think that you'll still be saved and love God if you "take a break." Don't fall for this trap. In the Bible, Paul admonishes us not to forsake the community of the church.
- Your children and family need church as much as you do. Your and their spirituality is more important than anything else.

o   The best thing for your children is to see you (and your spouse) following after Christ. This includes going to church. Show your children that God comes first in your life. Let them see how you overcome rejection by putting it behind and being the better person. Trust me, they're watching you and learning how to behave.

### *Mary*

> *And the angel said unto her, Fear not, Mary: for thou hast found favor with God. And, behold, thou shalt conceive in thy womb, and bring forth a son, and shalt call his name JESUS. He shall be great, and shall be called the Son of the Highest: and the Lord God shall give unto him the throne of his father David: And he shall reign over the house of Jacob for ever; and of his kingdom there shall be no end. Then said Mary unto the angel, How shall this be, seeing I know not a man? And the angel answered and said unto her, The Holy Ghost shall come upon thee, and the power of the Highest shall overshadow thee: therefore also that holy thing which shall be born of thee shall be called the Son of God. And, behold, thy cousin Elisabeth, she hath also conceived a son in her old age: and this is the sixth month with her, who was called barren. For with God nothing shall be impossible. And Mary said, Behold the handmaid of the Lord; be it unto me according to thy word. And the angel departed from her. And Mary arose in those days, and went into the hill country with haste, into a city of Judah.*
> *Luke 1: 30–39*

In Biblical times, it was scandalous to become pregnant outside of marriage. If it happened, the girl could be stoned to death out in the city streets. The public execution could possibly be started by the man to whom the girl was espoused. Mary, being a virgin, espoused to Joseph, faced quite the predicament. In this situation it's important to understand that Mary did not get her condition because of wrong choices. However, Mary must have anticipated the community's disapproval because the Bible said that she left in haste. The book of Matthew lets us know that there had to be some contention because Joseph was going to put her away.

This predicament put Mary in a dangerous position. This was more than just gossip and judgmental glances. Mary's condition, especially since it was outside of marriage, would bring about public shaming and possible death (remember the woman caught in adultery in John chapter 8).

One of the key players of this story is Joseph. He would have been well within his rights to cast Mary aside, to end their engagement, and to even drag her to her execution. The community would have completely supported him. Joseph's decisions would greatly affect Mary. This goes to show that leaders within the community should not take their influence lightly. The community probably waited on the word from Joseph as to what to do about the impregnated girl.

God made sure that Joseph understood the situation. After the dream, Joseph decided to believe Mary's story and support her. How shocked the community must have been! Some might have even been disappointed (oftentimes there are those who relish in someone else's demise). Joseph married Mary, and together they raised the Messiah.

### Final Thoughts

If you've been rejected by a community of people, the feeling of isolation is right there with you. But don't believe the lie of the enemy. You are not alone.

> *Be strong and of a good courage, fear not, nor be afraid*
> *of them: for the LORD thy God, he it is that doth go with*
> *thee; he will not fail thee, nor forsake thee.*
> *Deuteronomy 31:6*

Sometimes it's best to remove yourself from the situation and reflect and process the goals and purpose of the community. It could be that you have outgrown the group, or that your ideologies and plans for the future do not line up with the group. In this case, you may see the isolation as a rejection and feel dejected. It doesn't have to be this way. God could be calling you out and moving you to another level. That's exactly what happened with Mary. God took her out of a community in order to prepare her for her God-ordained journey.

Even if you feel that the community was helping you, and you were a good fit, God can take the situation and use it to open another door for you.

# CHAPTER TEN

## *Rejected by Society*
## *Esther*

Millions of Christians face persecution because of their faith.*
Christianity is the most widely persecuted religion in the world.*
News reports of Christians forced to line up in the streets to be
shot, or dragged out of their homes only to have their heads cut
off, shock us and shake us to our core.

In America, we are blessed with the freedom to worship, and
our lives are normally not on the line, but the persecution still
comes at us. Right now it's a battle of words and ideologies. But
it can still lead to rejection, especially when choosing to stand for
your faith in the face of opposition.

*Why?*

We want to fit in. Most of us don't like making waves. So, we
keep quiet and live our Christianity in a way so that it doesn't
bother others.

As a young girl attending public school, I had a difficult time
dealing with my differences due to my family's religion. Wearing

skirts every day posed a problem for a tomboy like me who enjoyed the monkey bars. Mom would make me culottes to keep me modest, but it didn't help with my popularity.

When I got into high school, I learned to adjust. I'd hang out with my school friends and act like them (like smoking cigarettes in the bathroom), then go to church on Sunday and act like the good church girl I was supposed to be. My sisters even took it a step further, changing into pants once they got to school. But how many souls did I win to the Lord? Probably none. In all honesty, I'm not sure. I was too busy trying to fit in and not be rejected by a society that didn't understand me or my faith.

Societal pressures do exist, and they don't go away as we get older. It's a larger canvas of community. But rejection is just as prevalent for those of us willing to stand out and be different.

This can be seen in today's American culture. Hot topics of acceptance and tolerance travel through the air waves and are having lasting effects in our churches and our spiritual lives. Many of our decisions are often made because we fear the rejection of our society.

When we stand upon the principles of God and His Word, we may at some point have to deal with the backlash of society. There are several terms that they throw at us, none of them with a positive connotation: hypocrites, judgmental Christians, believers of fairytales, Jesus freaks, ignorant sheep.

To make matters worse, we sometimes face rejection from other fellow believers. So, we don't fit in with the worldly philosophies of our society, yet we struggle to fit in as well with the community of believers.

Being rejected by society can be too isolating, but government powers can do a lot more than hurt our feelings. They can take away freedoms and possibly endanger those who don't follow their laws. It's something we don't think a lot about here in America where our liberties and freedoms are easily taken for granted. But

I urge you to ask yourself: are you willing to be rejected for the cause of Christ? No matter the outcome?

### Esther

> *Then Mordecai commanded to answer Esther, Think not with thyself that thou shalt escape in the king's house, more than all the Jews. For if thou altogether holdest thy peace at this time, then shall there enlargement and deliverance arise to the Jews from another place; but thou and thy father's house shall be destroyed: and who knoweth whether thou art come to the kingdom for such a time as this? Then Esther bade them return Mordecai this answer, Go, gather together all the Jews that are present in Shushan, and fast ye for me, and neither eat nor drink three days, night or day: I also and my maidens will fast likewise; and so will I go in unto the king, which is not according to the law: and if I perish, I perish.*
>
> *Esther 4:13–16*

The Biblical story of Esther is inspiring. A Jewish girl chosen to be queen stands up for her God and her people in the face of death. She comes out triumphant and saves the Jews from a horrific end. Sounds glorious, doesn't it?

But step into her shoes for a minute. She's taken from her home, forced to marry a king who she had barely met, finds out her cousin has infuriated the king's right-hand man, and now the entire Jewish nation could face a possible extermination. She may be queen, but she has no say. She can't even approach the king without his invitation without the risk of punishment.

Her heritage and people were rejected by her king at the hands of an evil, vengeful vizier. And if they found out about her, would she share the same fate?

The Jewish people had already endured so much. They were dispelled as a nation hundreds of years before Esther, faced captivity at the hands of Babylon, and were scattered still across Palestine and Persia. Nehemiah, who would eventually lead the Israelites back to Jerusalem and the rebuilding of its city walls, was the generation after Esther. What does that imply?

Esther's actions contributed to God's ultimate purpose for His people. But she had to face rejection against a society that wanted her and her people dead. Without Esther's actions and accomplishments, the Hebrews would have faced massive persecution and torture in that region and ultimately changed the course of events.

All Esther had to do was make the choice to avoid the potential rejection. By accepting the risk, she had to have had moments of doubt, even moments of fear. We can say that we would have done the same thing, but would we?

The situation was dire. Haman, the king's vizier, was second in command. He had a problem with Mordechai—Esther's elder cousin who actually cared for her after her parents' death—because Mordechai refused to bow when Haman came near. Haman's pride took over, and rage and vengeance fueled him to manipulate King Xerxes into issuing the destruction of the Jews.

Haman wouldn't be satisfied with only hurting Mordechai, he determined that all of the Jewish people needed to be killed. He justified it to the king by pointing out how the Jews were "foreign" with different customs and beliefs.

> *And Haman said unto king Ahasuerus, There is a certain people*
> *scattered abroad and dispersed among the people in all the provinces*
> *of thy kingdom; and their laws are diverse from all people; neither*
> *keep they the king's laws: therefore it is not for the king's profit to*
> *suffer them. If it please the king, let it be written that they may be*
> *destroyed: and I will pay ten thousand talents of silver to the hands*
> *of those that have the charge of the business, to bring it into the*
> *king's treasuries. And the king took his ring from his hand, and gave*
> *it unto Haman the son of Hammedatha the Agagite, the Jews' enemy.*
> *And the king said unto Haman, The silver is given to thee, the people*
> *also, to do with them as it seemeth good to thee.*
>
> *Esther 3:8–11*

The only hope the Jewish people had rested in their queen. Esther, however, didn't see it that way. She knew she could not approach her husband and casually say, "Hey, honey, just thought you should know that your right-hand man is evil and is plotting against my people. Oh, did I forget to mention that I'm a Jew? Sorry about that. Just the same, could you ease up on the whole Jewish extermination?"

This matter could not be taken lightly. Esther at first told Mordechai that she couldn't help. She saw the situation as hopeless. What power did she have to sway the king? But Mordechai left her no choice, basically telling her, "You have to try. If you don't do this, who will?"

Esther eventually agreed, but she doesn't mince words. "I'll do it, but I might die."

Now she faced quite the dilemma. She needed to figure out a way to expose Haman without risking her life or putting her people more at risk. But how could any of that be accomplished if the king didn't invite her into his presence?

So, now Esther faced *two* potential rejections. One: if the king determined that the Jewish people should not be saved. Two: if the king rejected his wife in the first place.

Talk about pressure!

Can you imagine her thought process?

*Surely, he won't order me killed ... but what if he does?*

*He chose me as his wife, that's got to mean something ... then again, he had no problem getting rid of his last wife!*

*What if he rejects me in front of everyone?*

*Does he love me enough? Maybe he does! Oh, no, maybe he doesn't! Will he kill me right on the spot?*

*What if Haman finds out about me and tells the king before I do?*

Esther pushed past any doubts and she entered into the throne room of the king. Uninvited. And totally exposed. Because of that, Esther saved her people.

### Final Thoughts

I've heard it said that living for God in today's times isn't easy. The world's system oftentimes conflicts with God's. For example, the world says that living together before marriage is a great idea—take that time and test each other out—but God's Word says otherwise. Or, marrying an unbeliever may be no big deal when observing the world's standards, but God's system says differently.

We find ourselves asking questions like:

- Is it okay if I drink alcohol as long as I don't get drunk?
- How far can I go with my boyfriend before it gets too far?
- Is modesty really that big of a deal to God?
- Can I chat with the man online without it being cheating?

- Attendance to church every Sunday isn't critical to my salvation, is it?

The problem with these types of questions is that we begin confusing the world's standards with God's. Before long, we question a lot more. Then our prayer life—already on life support—crashes and dies. We tout our Christianity like a badge, but only for appearance's sake, and only if it's convenient.

Why is this? Could it be that we are trying desperately to protect ourselves from the rejection of society? Caving in hurts less, right? It feels good to party with coworkers or to make a few questionable love connections. What's the big deal? But by trying to protect yourself from rejection, you are ultimately rejecting the One who's promised to be faithful.

Not only that, but blending the world's standards with God's is like mixing oil and water. They don't mix. Eventually, one is going to win out. Jesus warned us of this: no one can serve two masters.

So what if we choose God and His Word? What if we decide that rejection by society is the price to pay for our relationship with God? Simply this: be ready to not fit in.

To unbelievers we don't make a lot of sense. Even more than that, we are criticized for being narrow-minded, hypocritical, prejudiced, and judgmental. It seems if anyone dissents or merely raises a question about today's prevailing thoughts or agendas, they are to be ostracized and publicly ridiculed.

The Bible states that this separation of ideals shouldn't surprise us:

> *Marvel not, my brethren, if the world hate you.*
> *I John 3:13*

Not only does the Bible indicate that serving God is not going to mesh with the worldly mindset of others, but it also points out that rejection is going to take place. It's already a given.

> *Yea, and all that will live godly in*
> *Christ Jesus shall suffer persecution.*
> *2 Timothy 3:12*

So, if we are already going to be rejected by society, where does God fit in? The answer can be found in the book of Mark:

> *And ye shall be hated of all men for my name's sake:*
> *but he that shall endure unto the end,*
> *the same shall be saved.*
> *Mark 13:13*

The fact is that we may be rejected by society. This is especially true when we make the decision to stand for God and His statutes. Just remember that the world is no match for our Savior. Jesus has already won.

# CHAPTER ELEVEN

## *Rejected by Circumstances*
## *Hannah*

It was Tuesday, and I had endured another stressful day in the school district. I drove up our driveway, parked the car outside the garage, then made my way to the house.

"Hey, Jay!" Mom called through the window of her apartment. "Want to run to the store?"

"Not right now," I said without masking the annoyance in my voice. I didn't even bother to glance up. I walked straight into my house and shut the door.

Mom had come to live with us six years earlier. After being laid off, she had nowhere to go, so she sold her house, packed up, and moved in with me and my family. With the extra money from the sale of her house, she paid for an apartment and garage to be built on our property. That way, she wouldn't have to worry about bills or taxes.

Normally I enjoyed the arrangement. Mom might have driven my husband crazy a time or two, but she and I had grown closer. She cultivated gardens in my yard I never had without her. She would pray for anything I went to her about. She'd cook for the boys, then call them up to her apartment for dinner.

But Mom had the habit of pouncing on me the minute I'd get home from work. I had tried to explain that I needed to unwind for a while, but there was always a reason she needed or wanted to talk.

I had yet to take off my shoes when she opened the door to my house and walked in.

I don't remember what she said. Something about work and some of the things she had accomplished that day. Just small talk.

But I remember my words perfectly. "Mom, I'm really tired. Can you please give me some time alone?"

Mom apologized and left.

Those were the last words I ever spoke to her.

The next day I went to work, taught my classes, came home. It was Wednesday.

My friend texted me and asked what happened to my mother because she never showed up to volunteer at the radio station. It sounded odd. Mom never missed an important meeting or date. I texted her, but there was no response.

John, my husband, was already outside waiting for me to go to Bible study.

"Have you seen Mom today?" I asked from the screen door.

"No, but I thought I saw her car in the garage."

My stomach immediately dropped to my feet as the sense of foreboding sent red flags waving in my brain. I ran into the garage, saw her car, and ran to the stairway that led to her apartment.

The stench hit my nostrils immediately. "No, no, no, no, no, no, no...!" was what I remember saying.

The smell of human excrement nauseatingly increased as I rushed into her bedroom.

My world, at that moment, came crashing to a standstill.

There lay my mother, face down on the carpet beside her bed. "Mom? *Mom!*"

I screamed for my husband, then began praying. "Please, God, I beg you. Don't take her. Not like this."

The carpet was soaked. Her pajamas were ruined. Yet, my husband, seeing me frozen in the bedroom, tried to resuscitate her.

"Call 9-1-1!" he said, snapping me out of my shock. "She's still breathing!"

I moved quickly, making the necessary phone calls and praying in between each call. I contacted my siblings explaining the direness of the situation, then my father, then my pastor. Down through the list. All the while praying that God would save my mother's life.

The ambulance arrived, and I rushed to be alongside my mom. I stood outside the ER room as they began life support for her. I sat by her side the entire night holding her hand, singing her songs, and praying. She continued to lay in a coma, completely unresponsive.

At some point, and I'm unsure the time, I had her hand in mine, and was listening to the beeping of the machines. In that quiet moment, I whispered, "Please, God...."

In a still, small voice, I heard the words, "I have called her home."

Feeling the presence of God in a powerful way, I bowed my head and sobbed.

Because in that moment when God spoke to me, I had never felt more rejected in my life.

\* \* \*

What do you do when God says no? How do you handle the tumultuous feelings of loneliness and grief when God seemingly fails to show up?

I was angry after Mom died. First, I was angry at myself. The guilt weighed heavily upon me that I had rejected spending time with my mother just the day before. Then I played the grief-stricken game of "If-Only":

- If only I had spent some quality time with her....
- If only I had bought her that emergency response necklace....
- If only I called her earlier in the morning....
- If only I had checked on her more regularly....
- If only I had told her I love her....
- If only I had hugged her neck one more time....

Then I became angry with God. If He's real, why didn't He just heal her? Why'd He let it happen in the first place? Doesn't the Bible say that by His stripes we're healed? But more than all of those questions, it bothered me that I felt rejected by the circumstances. Simply put, I felt rejected by God.

In my mind, the one who was supposed to help didn't. The one who was supposed to watch over my mom like He watches over sparrows didn't. The one who was supposed to listen to my cry and attend unto my plea didn't.

I struggled with how to cope with these jarring contradictions. As I moved through the days following in a fog—dealing with family conflict and memorial arrangements and contacting a funeral home—I needed God more than ever, yet I would remind myself how He let me down.

I gave a beautiful memorial speech honoring my mother and her walk with God. I said the words, but my heart choked on them.

During the night I would cry myself to sleep.

At the school district, I would put the façade firmly in place while the administration attacked me and gave me poor reviews.

When I attended church I would sit there feeling completely empty inside.

One day as I was going through Mom's things, I picked up her Bible and small notebook that she kept beside her chair in the living room. Her Bible had been read many times over and was filled with her notes and markings. I sat and read her words and felt the overwhelming peace of God. As I sat in her chair reading her Bible, I began to unload my hurt and despair out loud. I told God exactly how I felt. How I felt that He let me down. How He could have easily healed her. I asked why He let it happen to begin with, and didn't He realize how much I needed my mom in my life?

I'm not sure how long I sat in the quiet apartment tearfully venting at God, but I felt His presence there in a most beautiful way. I felt reassured that He understood me and felt my anguish, too.

Circumstances happen that are oftentimes completely outside of our control. This makes our vulnerability all the more real. Even though we will feel the pain of rejection and the discomfort that it brings, there is peace to be found.

I know because I eventually found it.

### Hannah

> *And [Elkanah] had two wives; the name of the one was Hannah, and*
> *the name of the other Peninnah: and Peninnah had children,*
> *but Hannah had no children.*
>
> *And this man went up out of his city yearly to worship and to*
> *sacrifice unto the LORD of hosts in Shiloh. And the two sons of Eli,*

> *Hophni and Phinehas, the priests of the* Lord, *were there. And when*
> *the time was that Elkanah offered, he gave to Peninnah his wife, and*
> *to all her sons and her daughters, portions:*
> *But unto Hannah he gave a worthy portion; for he loved Hannah:*
> *but the* Lord *had shut up her womb. And her adversary also*
> *provoked her sore, for to make her fret,*
> *because the* Lord *had shut up her womb.*
> *And as he did so year by year, when she went up to the house of the*
> Lord, *so she provoked her; therefore she wept, and did not eat.*
> *Then said Elkanah her husband to her, Hannah, why weepest thou?*
> *and why eatest thou not? and why is thy heart grieved? am not I*
> *better to thee than ten sons? So Hannah rose up after they had eaten*
> *in Shiloh, and after they had drunk ... And she was in bitterness of*
> *soul, and prayed unto the* Lord, *and wept sore.*
> *I Samuel 1:2–10*

You can feel Hannah's turmoil on the page. Day in and day out, she watched as Elkanah's other wife, Peninnah, had child after child. Not only did she have to share her husband's affections with this second women, Hannah had to be barren on top it. It wasn't that Elkanah didn't love her, or that he loved Peninnah more. Actually, Scripture makes a point to mention that he took care of Hannah and loved her, leading us to believe that he preferred her. But what Hannah wanted desperately, what she had pleaded to God for, she wasn't getting.

The Bible goes even further to state that Lord had "shut up her womb." So, the very God she was praying to was the one who was causing the situation to begin with.

But Hannah had had enough. Peninnah had provoked her one too many times. This time when she went up to the house of the Lord, she wept in bitterness and rejection and prayed a very specific prayer.

> *And she vowed a vow, and said, O LORD of hosts, if thou wilt indeed*
> *look on the affliction of thine handmaid, and remember me, and not*
> *forget thine handmaid, but wilt give unto thine handmaid a man*
> *child, then I will give him unto the LORD all the days of his life, and*
> *there shall no razor come upon his head.*
> *I Samuel 1:11*

Praying out of desperation, she asked God to look upon her torment and answer her prayer. Hannah goes on to offer the child back to the Lord. Basically, she tells God that if He gives her a boy baby, then she will — after he is weaned — give him to the service of the Lord. She must have been acting a little strange because Eli the priest thought she was drunk. Her response tells a different story.

> *And Hannah answered and said, No, my lord, I am a woman of a*
> *sorrowful spirit: I have drunk neither wine nor strong drink, but*
> *have poured out my soul before the LORD.*
> *I Samuel 1:15*

Hannah's answer connected with me. Many times I have poured my soul out before the Lord. I have even tried making deals with Him, like Hannah did. "Lord, if you do this, then I'll do this for you."

But God doesn't need us to play Let's Make A Deal. Nor does He need us to be reserved and formal when we approach Him. There are those of us who may think that God requires formality. He doesn't. You don't have to chant or do a special ritual to get

His attention. You don't have to be in a specific room in a specific position in order to channel an effective prayer. Just like with Hannah, He hears the cry of your heart. A verse in Psalms states:

> *The righteous cry, and the LORD heareth,*
> *and delivereth them out of all their troubles.*
> *Psalm 34:17*

Several verses into I Samuel chapter one, the Bible states that the Lord remembered Hannah. It wasn't that He had forsaken her or turned His back on her, but could it have been that He waited for the right time needed for the fulfillment of Samuel's ministry? Samuel is God's answer to Hannah's prayer. Samuel is also considered one of the greatest prophets of the Old Testament.

What would have happened if Hannah had been able to have children with no challenge? Would she have dedicated her firstborn, Samuel, to the Lord? Would she have reached a point where the only place she could turn was to God?

In this case, Hannah might have felt rejected by her circumstances, but God hadn't been saying no to her as much as He was saying, *not now.*

### Final Thoughts

Being rejected by circumstances, especially those outside of your control, can become overwhelming and can lead to doubt, worry, and anxiety. We worry because we don't know what's going to happen or why it's happening, or we struggle with understanding the how and why of events in the first place. Worry then leads to anxiety and possibly depression. Hannah most likely struggled with some form of depression. It had to get tiring to go year after year and watch God bless her antagonist while seemingly ignoring her.

I have a hard time understanding why God doesn't come through for me, especially when I need Him. In all honesty, I have felt rejected by my circumstances more times than I can probably count. The reason behind that could simply be that I like to be in control. I struggle not to become frustrated or all bent-out-of-shape when something doesn't go according to my plan and effort. Somehow, it becomes God's fault.

Yet, God reminds us that His agenda isn't exactly ours.

> *For my thoughts are not your thoughts, neither are your ways my ways, saith the LORD. For as the heavens are higher than the earth, so are my ways higher than your ways, and my thoughts than your thoughts.*
> Isaiah 55:8–9

Even if you have been rejected by circumstances, you can still find peace. I did. When I read through my mother's Bible, I was encouraged by her faithfulness. I felt that blessed assurance that my mother might no longer be with me physically, but her life is far from over. Knowing her, she is probably shouting up and down the streets of gold, worshipping God. She no longer has to struggle with the cares of this life. My mom went home and earned her reward.

I might not understand why it had to be so soon. I might still question why it had happened the way it did. But I have made a conscious choice not to be rejected by the circumstances of her death. I may not understand God, but I trust Him. I may not be in control, but He is.

And there's peace in the knowing.

# *Part Three:*
# *Break Free!*

*Stand fast therefore in the liberty wherewith Christ hath made us free, and be not entangled again with the yoke of bondage.*

*~Galatians 5:1*

# CHAPTER TWELVE

## *Breaking Free: The Truth about Rejection*

For years I acted like a victim because of rejection. I wallowed in the hurt and fought against the bitterness. I didn't want the negative feelings to consume me. I became very good at pretending. Yet, I struggled spiritually because of my brokenness. That is until I turned it over to God and sought healing.

I knew I couldn't live life constantly wondering if someone liked me, or if they didn't like me, worrying about why. Did I do something wrong? Maybe it's the way I look?

Sometimes I would blame God. Why do I always have to get rejected? Why do I have to be the one that gets hurt?

Eventually I said, *Enough!* It unfortunately took the death of my mother to wake me up. I realized this is the only life God has given me to be a blessing on this earth. And I was squandering it by focusing on other people's rejection of me.

In order to break free from rejection, we have to understand the truth about it. Think of it this way: you have to know your enemy. And yes, rejection is your enemy.

What is the definition of an enemy? Someone or something acting hostile, causing conflict. Another definition is someone or something weakening you or trying to hurt you. Sound like rejection?

Before countries or kingdoms would go off to war, there would be numerous strategy sessions to figure out the best plan of action that would result in *victory*. Many a battle was won—not necessarily on the ground—but in the strategy meetings before the battle. One tactic used was learning about the enemy. What were the enemy's strengths and weaknesses? By knowing and understanding who they were fighting, commanders of the army would be able to make educated decisions that would result in *the enemy's defeat*.

This war tactic is still used today. And it needs to be utilized in spiritual warfare as well.

When you start to feel the negative effects of rejection—no matter the cause—know it for what it is. We're human, and we're living in a flawed world, which means that the enemy is going to continue to throw rejection our way. However, we can nip it from soaking into the soil of our heart and spreading its roots.

### Truths about Rejection

1. Rejection is a tool of the enemy.

Rejection is a tool used by Satan himself to defeat you and keep you in spiritual chains. The Bible specifically calls the devil our enemy.

> *Your adversary the devil, as a roaring lion,*
> *walketh about, seeking whom he may devour.*
> I Peter 5:8

Trust me he's not trying to be your friend. He wants you to feel anxious and upset, and worried and sad. More than that, he wants to pull you away from your Heavenly Father and His protection. The more you allow yourself to stay chained to the negative feelings of rejection, the longer you stay in the clutches of your enemy.

The devil doesn't show up on your doorstep and ask to come in. He knows that would never happen. So what does he do? He plays mind games with us. He whispers in our thoughts how unworthy we are ... that it's our fault ... that there's something wrong with us ... that we're not lovable ... that we don't deserve forgiveness or a second chance. The list goes on and on, but the point is that he already knows our weaknesses and he uses that knowledge to push us down into continued despair, loneliness, and/or bitterness.

If you are currently feeling defeated because of someone else's actions or response to you, then you are exactly where the enemy wants you. Because of rejection, we turn within ourselves to lick our wounds. However, by becoming self-absorbed—even if it is because of rejection—our eyes and focus are off the one who is our remedy. Satan distracts us. Don't think about how good God is. Don't remember all the times He's been there for you and brought you through. Oh, no, focus on the pain of the "now." Dwell on the hurt and anger. Unfortunately, if we're not careful, we'll build a wall between us and God.

Are you listening to the voice of the enemy?

- Do you walk around with a constant chip on your shoulder?
- Do you have trouble forgiving others, even for the slightest offence?

- Do you find yourself becoming angry often?
- Do you sabotage relationships with hurtful words or actions?
- Do you feel overwhelmed by despair? Depression? Loneliness? Abandonment? Bitterness? *Rejection*?

If you find yourself answering yes to any of the above questions, it's time you recognize your real enemy and cut him off.

2. Rejection doesn't feel good.

Of course it doesn't feel good, right? I've never met a person who embraces rejection with open arms. The key, however, is that it doesn't feel good for *anyone*. That doesn't give us a pass on behaving badly or suffering internally because we've been hurt. It is God's desire and will for us to lead overcoming lives. That's hard to do when we refuse to get back up when we've been pushed down.

In order to know our enemy, we need to understand what rejection is and how it makes us feel, so that we can remove it from our lives.

- Rejection makes me feel:

_____

_____

_____

_____

_____

Now that we've been honest with ourselves, tell God how it makes you feel, then hand it over to Him. Before I was set free from the bondage of rejection, I had to be honest with God.

*Hey, God, it's me. I have to tell you something: I'm really hurting inside right now. I feel like I can't do anything right. No matter how hard*

*I try, I still feel attacked. I'm tired of crying and feeling like I'm not good enough. So, I'm handing this mess over to you.*

Yes, rejection hurts. But don't let the hurt build a house in your heart and stay! Kick it to the curb by handing it over to God. Trust me, God can handle it.

### 3. Rejection is not fair.

Have you ever wanted to throw a major temper tantrum?

My mother told me once how, when I was a toddler, my brother and sister would be playing a game of Candy Land, and I would march right over and sit in the middle of the board game. They'd push me aside and from there I would kick and scream. I didn't understand the game, yet I wanted to be right in the middle of it. From my parents and siblings' accounts, I threw tantrums quite a bit.

But we can't go through life like we're toddlers. Temper tantrums stop being tolerated once you pass a certain age. I've read articles and have observed on the news adults losing their cool and punching holes in walls or hurting someone else in a "fit of rage." This type of behavior is unacceptable and can lead to severe consequences.

Just the same, I'd be lying if I said I had never envisioned throwing a tantrum as an adult. Why? Because life's not fair. Because people can be mean for no reason. Because it's hard to deal with rejection when you don't know what you've done or how to fix it.

Here's the deal: you can be rejected even if you're doing everything you're supposed to be doing. While teaching at the middle school, I can honestly say that I did my job to the best of my ability. I wanted to make the other teachers and the principal happy. I wanted them to like me. I would arrive to work early. I would give of my time outside of school, expecting nothing in return. I would teach in the style that they pushed in the building. Yet, I would leave the job daily feeling deflated and undervalued.

I began to think that I must be doing something wrong. So I kept changing, trying to fit into the version of me my coworkers and administrator wanted. Now I can look back at that situation and see that there was absolutely nothing I could have done that would have actually changed things. For whatever reason, they didn't like me. Sure I was told that I had a strong personality, that I wasn't working as a team, and that I was pushy. But I had tried to rectify all of that. I became more submissive. I bit my tongue and kept my mouth shut instead of asking questions. I didn't want to come across as too strong, so I learned to keep silent. That didn't work either.

Now that I am a college instructor and am out of that toxic environment, I realize that I was not the one with the problem. How do I know that? Because those issues did not follow me. When my college administrator complimented me on being one of the best instructors she ever observed, I nearly fell out of my chair! I didn't know how to handle such a compliment. When I was asked by the college to give a keynote presentation at a community leadership meeting, I couldn't believe they would entrust me with such an honor. Then they asked me to lead in a series of professional development trainings. What I began to realize was that what happened at my earlier job was not my fault.

We can't force people to like us. Even people who should embrace you can turn on you and reject you. There have been those I thought were my close friends who turned against me. I have watched extended family members not speak to each other over some frivolous argument. I have even observed adult children ignore and hurt their own parents, or parents who have hurt or betrayed their children. If you've been a victim in any of these instances, please know that it might not be anything you've done. Rejection sometimes doesn't have a reason, and sometimes the reasons for rejection are the other person's issue … not yours.

If you do the best you can do and still get rejected, remember that rejection isn't fair. Proverbs 29:27 says that the wicked will "detest the upright." And Jesus said in Luke 21:17 that "Everyone will hate you because of me." This doesn't mean that we have a license to not change or grow. Of course not. We need to improve ourselves. However, if at the end of the day you have given your all and even gone so far as to try and accommodate others, then you can sleep knowing that their rejection of you is on them. You don't have to own it.

# CHAPTER THIRTEEN

## *Breaking Free: The Truth about Priorities*

We've become narcissistic. Don't believe me? How many times do we check Facebook? How many times do we pick up our phone to check messages or emails? How often do we take a selfie? How often do we 'look out for number one'? If not us, I'm sure we can come up with quite a few people who could fit the bill.

Self-absorption distorts the lens of reality. It shouts that everything is about you and your feelings. But, newsflash: it's not about you. To be fair, it's not about me either.

> *For of him, and through him, and to him, are all things:*
> *to whom be glory for ever. Amen.*
> *Romans 11:36*

The world doesn't give God the glory. The world's philosophy is to push people out of the way to get what you want, no matter the consequences. We prize accolades, no matter how small. We want to feel good, and we look to others to make sure it gets accomplished. We dress provocatively because it gets us attention. We hold the camera at an angle to capture our best side. And we're passing our self-absorbed ways onto our children.

Sure, some may exercise some restraint, but I'm sure we can think of a few times when we've been thrown under the bus so that someone else can push past us and get the credit. How does God get the glory in that?

As a society, we've become so self-absorbed that we place our needs and desires above others. We make money but aren't content. We enjoy superficial television shows while our own lives lack meaning. Happiness eludes us.

Why? Could it be because our priorities are out of line with the will and purpose of God?

> To the pure, all things are pure; but to those who are defiled
> and unbelieving, nothing is pure, but both their mind and
> their conscience are defiled. They profess to know God,
> but by their deeds they deny Him, being detestable and
> disobedient and worthless for any good deed.
> Titus 1:15–16

This becomes even more noticeable when we are injured inside. Depressed and isolated, thanks to some rejection, self-preservation becomes paramount. Because of that, we get stuck in our circumstances and can't see past the pain.

We may never be able to stop rejection from hurting. Just the same, rejection doesn't have to debilitate us. The key is to stop thinking about the situation and how badly we feel and instead keep our focus where it belongs.

> *For in him we live, and move, and have our being ...*
>
> *Acts 17:28*

If you want to break free from rejection, it's time for the negative cycle to stop. That's right. Shake yourself off and set your priorities in order.

1. Get Off the Throne of Your Heart

We have to stop being consumed with ourselves and our problems. The world doesn't revolve around us. It doesn't stop to feel our pain. It keeps going. This isn't meant to hurt anyone's feelings, but in order to overcome rejection, we have to stop giving it rental space in our hearts. We can become so distraught because of rejection that it becomes ruler of our lives. Everything we say, every decision we make, every thought comes through the negative lens of rejection.

Whether we want to admit it or not, we are allowing it to consume us. How do we do that?

- We grumble and complain.
- We focus on our problems.
- We let the rejection we're feeling affect other aspects of our lives.
- We have a hard time letting go and forgiving.

While working at the school district, I became a very negative person. I would complain to anyone willing to listen. I would put down my coworkers. I would gossip about them. I'd make fun of the administrator to my friends and family. When bad things happened in their lives, a part of me actually felt vindicated. Basically I had become so consumed with the pain of my own rejection that I became a person I didn't think I'd ever become—a bitter, cynical, sarcastic woman. I thought acting that way made me tough, that it would help me develop a thick skin. But rejection had turned me hateful.

All the while I attended church, taught Sunday school, and paid my tithe. I kept the façade going at work, smiling at those I despised. I didn't see anything wrong with my behavior. They were the ones who treated me poorly. They were the ones who pushed me to the point of breaking.

By focusing on the situation and all that I had to endure, my heart had hardened and had become angry. My husband mentioned it several times about how much I "hated" my job. He'd say, "You used to love teaching. Now you seem to hate everything about it."

Something finally clicked. The more I thought about it, the more I realized that I had allowed the rejection to consume me. I didn't want to be that angry, bitter person. I wanted to be a teacher who positively affected her students no matter how others treated me. As I prayed and sought God for help and clarity, He revealed my selfishness with one simple verse:

> *Finally, brethren, whatsoever things are true,*
> *whatsoever things are honest, whatsoever*
> *Things are just, whatsoever things are pure, whatsoever*
> *things are lovely, whatsoever things are of good report; if*
> *there be any virtue, and if there be any praise,*
> *think on these things.*
> *Philippians 4:8*

This verse convicted me because I knew my heart wasn't right. I had turned all my attention to myself and my rejection. What I should have been doing was turning it over to God. There's only room for one to sit on the throne of my heart. Jesus warns us that no one can serve two masters.

Not only should we only serve God alone, but by keeping Him on the throne of our heart, we are giving Him control. We look to Him when rejection occurs. We "cast our cares upon Him" when He is Lord of our life.

> *Looking unto Jesus, the author and finisher of our faith …*
> *Hebrews 12:2*

2.  Seek God First

If God is to sit on the throne in our lives, we have to seek Him first. We have to put aside self-absorbency and trying to figure out how to handle everything on our own. Why? Because we seem to make a mess when we try to take care of things ourselves.

> *Seek ye my face; my heart said unto thee,*
> *Thy face, Lord, will I seek.*
> *Psalm 27:8*

I learned this the hard way. When I was young I'd write in journals, I'd write poetry, and I'd write short stories. As a newly married twenty-something, I dabbled in writing suspense scenes, not really taking them much further. There was never a conversation between me and God about my love and talent for writing. It was just my hobby. I was twenty-seven when I first met a successful author. He was promoting his middle grade novel, and I was teaching middle school students, so I went to his session. The author and I talked one-on-one a bit, and he gave me some tips to getting published. He ended our conversation with, "Nothing will ever get published if you don't write and finish it."

I took his advice to heart and started writing seriously. Writing became more than just a hobby. It became my passion.

Others would shop to relieve stress or take bubble baths, I'd open up my laptop and write my stories. I'd go to conferences and get my work critiqued, but I kept hitting a wall when it came to a publisher offering me a contract. I've written and completed seven novels ... and not *one* of them has been published yet. With well over 200 rejections, the only prayer I was offering was a lot of begging. And a lot of questions. I have asked God many times if it would ever happen.

A few years back, I was lamenting about this to my sister. I told her I didn't understand why God was keeping all the doors shut. She simply asked, "Have you asked Him what He wants you to write?"

I was irritated because I had not one time actually asked God what He wanted me to write. And I didn't feel I needed to. I was the writer, and He gave me the talent. Didn't that give me permission to write what I wanted?

My dream to write had been mine. I hadn't shared it with God other than the "Please, please, please," prayers. Besides, wouldn't God be too busy with other more important issues? Still, my sister's words convicted me, and I sheepishly began to pray, "Lord, you gave me this passion and this talent. What is it you want me to write?"

And you are all reading the finished product of His answer.

Seeking God first is not only a Biblical command, but it honestly helps us save a lot of wasted time. It took me over a decade before I actually made God the Lord over *my everything*, including my dreams.

> *Seek the Lord and his strength:*
> *seek his face evermore.*
> Psalm 105:4

It took me an embarrassingly amount of time to realize that my dreams were just as important to God, and He would fulfill them in His time and for His purpose.

All of our hearts' desires are important to God. He cares about us more than we will ever understand. But He is a gentleman, and He will not come barging into our lives without an invitation. The Bible says that He stands at the door and knocks, but He leaves the decision of opening the door to us. Yet, if we want His perfect peace and the unspeakable joy that comes from the Holy Spirit, God must be first. He cannot come second to another.

You might be thinking, *God's already first in my life! I gave my heart to Him years ago!*

But do you seek Him first in *everything*?

- Does your day start with prayer?
- Do you talk to God about your rejections? Your fears? Your heartache?
- Do you study the Word to glean His wisdom?
- Do you honor God in your accomplishments?
- Do you seek God's direction before making a decision?
- Do you wait upon Him patiently, no matter how long it takes?

When God is first in our lives, our eyes are on Him. When He is our focus, our rejections don't seem nearly so wounding. Sure, they might sting. But when God is first, we are strong through Him. We have that blessed assurance of who we are in Him. The voices of the world and the adversary that tell us we're no good fade into the background as nothing but noise and empty words.

Renew your commitment to Jesus by laying it all at his feet. When God comes first in our lives, it puts everything else in its proper perspective. Our relationship with Him should be our first priority.

# CHAPTER FOURTEEN

## *Breaking Free: The Truth about Relationships*

Relationships suffer because of rejection. This happens when we internalize our hurt, as well as when we act out against others because of our hurt.

I'd come home from work so upset over the toxicity of the environment that I would lash out at my family members as soon as I walked in the door. I had to fight my angry words back, reminding myself that my husband and my sons had not rejected or mistreated me. Yet, sometimes it would still happen. I would take my frustrations out on the people I adored.

My last words to my mother were me snapping at her to give me some space.

Relationships are beautiful treasures from God, and I have paid a high price to learn and honor that.

I know it may seem that the world is against us, but there are those who love and support us. The pain of rejection can affect them, too, if we are not careful to protect the precious relationships God has given us.

We might think that we're strong enough to keep all of our hurts and anxieties to ourselves, but are we?

- We might have trust issues because we're trying to protect ourselves from getting hurt again. Yet, these trust issues can sabotage potential relationships.
- We snap at our family members because internalizing our pain from rejection weighs heavily upon us.
- Sometimes we treat the people who love us poorly because we have a hard time believing anyone could love us.
- We become bitter at those who have wronged us.
- We seek vengeance and retaliation in order to make ourselves feel better.
- We put on a tough façade so that no one sees our pain.

Take it from me and the hard lesson I learned: we are only on this earth for a short time. Don't waste one minute of it wallowing in rejection or defeat. Focus on developing the relationships you do have.

### Don't Give Up on Your Relationship with God

Just as I discussed in the last chapter, keep God first. Your relationship with Him will keep you secure through the storms of life. My life has been a complete mess at times, and I have weathered my share of storms. Yet, I learned a long time ago that my relationship with God would be the most important of my life. The reason why I am standing on the other side of rejection victorious is because I never let go of God's unchanging hand.

> *For I the LORD thy God will hold thy right hand,*
>
> *saying unto thee,*
>
> *Fear not; I will help thee.*
>
> *Isaiah 41:13*

It doesn't matter who's hurt us. It doesn't matter if the church or church leaders have let us down. God doesn't change. He promised to be the lover of our soul. He promised to be faithful. He loves us with an everlasting love.

> *Your steadfast love, O Lord, extends to the heavens,*
>
> *your faithfulness to the clouds.*
>
> *Psalm 36:5*

When we have a strong relationship with God, we see things as He sees them. We realize that all things work together for the good to them that love God and are called according to His purpose (Romans 8:28).

### Don't Take It Out on Those around You

We have to be careful not to lash out at others because we are hurting on the inside. The Bible provides several Scriptures that warn us to be careful that we don't allow our frustrations to attack others.

> *Be angry, and sin not: let not the sun go down upon your wrath.*
>
> *Ephesians 4:26*

In Proverbs, it says that a soft answer turns away wrath (Proverbs 15:1). That means that we shouldn't necessarily return anger for anger. If we're not careful, our hurtful words can negatively affect others.

> *Set a guard, O Lord, over my mouth;*
> *keep watch over the door of my lips!*
> *Psalm 141:3*

My mother would tell me to think twice before I speak and save myself a lot of heartache! Coming up with words and using them has never been an issue for me. My problem has always been knowing when to keep my mouth shut. I have had to apologize many times for lashing out at others when I was stressed or frustrated.

Remember that it hurts to be rejected, so don't allow our words and actions to reject others. We can wound our children with our words, hurt our marriages and our relationships with true friends by not keeping control over our tongues.

> *Let the words of my mouth and the meditation of my*
> *heart be acceptable in your sight,*
> *O Lord, my rock and my redeemer.*
> *Psalm 19:14*

## Forgive

Unforgiveness stems from rejection. When we refuse to forgive, we open the door for bitterness and other ugly roots to grow in our hearts. Our relationships with those around us could also suffer when we choose not to forgive. We owe it to ourselves and to those we love and care about to free ourselves of the chains of unforgiveness. Not to mention the Bible says that we must get rid of it.

> *Let all bitterness, and wrath, and anger, and clamor, and*
> *evil speaking, be put away from you, with all malice: And*
> *be ye kind one to another, tenderhearted, forgiving one*
> *another, even as God for Christ's sake hath forgiven you.*
> *Ephesians 4:31–32*

We can't be right with God when we have unforgiveness in our hearts. Not only that, but when we choose not to forgive, we block God's forgiveness upon our own lives.

> *For if ye forgive men their trespasses,*
> *your heavenly Father will also forgive you:*
> *But if ye forgive not men their trespasses,*
> *neither will your*
> *Father forgive your trespasses.*
> *Matthew 6:14–15*

Yes, it hurts to be rejected. Our flesh may want to harbor the hurt, but unforgiveness will keep us shackled in chains. Jesus desires to break the chains of rejection, but we hold onto the chains, the longer we choose to not forgive.

Then again, when our relationship with Jesus is the forefront of our life, we're ready to tackle forgiveness. We are reminded through His sacrifice that we are imperfect, too. The same Jesus who died for our sins is the same Jesus who died for others.

Forgiving ourselves is just as important as forgiving others. Sometimes our wrong actions can cause the negative consequences of rejection. Beating ourselves up only keeps us defeated. When I got kicked out of Bible College, I struggled for months with guilt, and I felt I was also rejected by God. I built the wall between Him and me because I had yet to forgive myself.

> *If we confess our sins, he is faithful and just to forgive us*
> *our sins, and to cleanse us from all unrighteousness.*
> *I John 1:9*

When we confess our sins, God forgives us. If He forgives us, then we should forgive ourselves and free our minds and hearts from the guilt and regret. By doing so, we free ourselves from the negative feelings that have kept us shackled.

## Let It Go

This can be challenging because rejection likes to rear its ugly head every now and then. While writing this book, I had to remember events that I had worked hard to push down and bury deep. I immediately went to God, asking for Him to help me once again let the pain of rejection go. The Bible goes so far to tell us that we need to pray God's blessings on those who have hurt us.

> *But I say unto you, Love your enemies, bless them that*
> *curse you, do good to them that hate you, and pray for*
> *them which despitefully use you, and persecute you;*
> *Matthew 5:44*

Letting it go—the past hurts, anger, bitterness—is the only way to truly move forward in life. By releasing the hurt that others have caused, we become free to enjoy the relationships of those who have not rejected us. And they deserve the best of us, not the leftovers.

The only way to let it go is to give it to Jesus. We don't have to bear the burden of rejection anymore. We don't have to lash out at others because we are suffering internally. God's purpose can be revealed no matter our past. But we can't hold on to what other people have done to us and still move toward God's destiny for our life.

That's not fair to us or our families. By learning to forgive and let go, we release ourselves to better, stronger relationships: with God, with our families, with our friends, and with ourselves.

# CHAPTER FIFTEEN

## *Breaking Free:*
## *The Truth about Yourself*

Sometimes we have the best of intentions. We want to forgive. We want strong relationships. We desire to know God intimately. But no matter how hard we try, we can't get past how we see ourselves. We fight past our insecurities, yet they continue to stare us in the face. We act like we don't care what others think about us, yet we let their negative words replay in our minds.

I can remember the boy who called me fat when I was in fifth grade. I've believed that about myself ever since. That's right. The words of a ten-year-old boy still replay in my mind.

The fact remains that if we want to be free from rejection, we have to start believing the truth about ourselves. We choose to be free from the chains of rejection. We make the choice daily how we're going to think about ourselves and how we are going to act—or react—when life happens.

In three of the gospels, we are introduced to a woman who was desperate for a change in her life. Matthew, Mark, and Luke all describe the scene that happened between the woman with the issue of blood and her encounter with Jesus. She had to have recognized that she could not get better on her own.

She recognized her need for Jesus and made a choice that changed her entire life:

> *And a woman having an issue of blood twelve years, which had spent all her living upon physicians, neither could be healed of any, Came behind him, and touched the border of his garment: and immediately her issue of blood stanched. And Jesus said, Who touched me? When all denied, Peter and they that were with him said, Master, the multitude throng thee and press thee, and sayest thou, Who touched me? And Jesus said, Somebody hath touched me: for I perceive that virtue is gone out of me. And when the woman saw that she was not hid, she came trembling, and falling down before him, she declared unto him before all the people for what cause she had touched him, and how she was healed immediately. And he said unto her, Daughter, be of good comfort: thy faith hath made thee whole; go in peace.*
>
> *Luke 8:43–48*

This woman had been sick for years. She had spent all her time and resources on doctors. She made a choice that day. Word must have spread around her town that the man named Jesus would be passing through. She had no doubt heard Him and the amazing miracles. The gospel of Matthew shows us her actual thoughts:

> *For she said within herself, If I may but touch*
> *his garment, I shall be whole.*
> Matthew 9:21

These passages give me chills every time I read them! What would have happened if she had accepted the rejection from the physicians and other well-meaning people who walked away from her because they had no answer for her condition? I'm sure doubt crossed her mind. *Do I really want to push through the crowds? I probably won't even be able to see Him. The rumors are probably exaggerated.*

But the woman set her doubts aside. She had a desperate need and was willing to recognize that she could not solve the problem on her own.

The crowds were pushing against Jesus. The whole town must have showed up, seeking a glimpse of the Nazarene to see if the rumors were true. Many showed up searching for a miracle. This woman, once again, must have doubts. *How do I know?* Because she had to encourage herself to keep moving forward. "If I can just touch the hem of his garments...."

Recognizing her need for Jesus saved her life. She had decided she didn't want to waste one more minute being sick. She believed the same Jesus who was healing others would do the same for her.

Her faith got Jesus' attention.

### We Need to Recognize Our Need for Jesus

This is the first truth about ourselves we've got to grasp. We need Jesus. I tried living life without Him. I tried juggling everything on my own. I tried to handle the stress and instead fought a failing battle with depression and heartache all by myself. In my head, I didn't want to burden God with the trivial things of my life. I would tell myself that I was too sensitive. That I needed to suck it up and learn to deal with the onslaught of negativity and hurtful words.

Here's the deal: it's okay to admit that we don't have it all together. I'll be the first to raise my hand. When I finally figured out that I needed God to help me feel whole again, I felt His love and peace in a profound way. It was then I understood that God desires us to come to Him. He's waiting for us to run to Him, to admit that we can't handle the rejection on our own.

> But he said to me, "My grace is sufficient for you, for my power is made perfect in weakness." Therefore I will boast all the more gladly of my weaknesses, so that the power of Christ may rest upon me.
>
> II Corinthians 12:9

Paul is saying that he freely admits that he is weak and in need of a Savior. There's nothing wrong with going to God and handing Him our burdens. He wants to come to our aid, but He is waiting on us to ask Him. We have to be able to admit just how much we need Him. When we recognize this about ourselves, God will show up and touch our lives in ways we never imagined.

### We Are Not a Surprise or a Mistake to God

> For you formed my inward parts; you knitted me together in my mother's womb. I praise you, for I am fearfully and wonderfully made. Wonderful are your works; my soul knows it very well. My frame was not hidden from you, when I was being made in secret, intricately woven in the depths of the earth. Your eyes saw my unformed substance; in your book were written, every one of them, the days that were formed for me, when as yet there was none of them.
>
> Psalm 139:13–16

God knows us by name. He even knows the number of hairs upon our head! He knew us when we were still in our mother's womb! Whoa!

Do we fully understand what that means? It means *divine destiny*. God has a purpose for us to be on this earth. You and I are not a mistake. We didn't just "happen" to show up on this planet by some freak coincidence.

> For I know the plans I have for you, declares the LORD, plans for welfare [your good] and not for evil, to give you a future and a hope.
>
> *Jeremiah 29:11*

It doesn't matter how many times we've been hurt through rejection. God still has a plan for us. And that plan does not involve us wallowing in despair. And let me add that there's nothing we could ever do, think, or say that would surprise God. He's not surprised by our personalities or what makes us happy or annoyed.

So don't lie to yourself with "It would be better if I'd have never been born!" Don't insult God or yourself like that. Realize that God has us here—each of us—for a very specific purpose. That doesn't mean the storms won't come or that people will necessarily stop being petty and hurtful. What it does mean is that God will bring us through it. And each storm and trial will only make us that much stronger and more resilient, especially when Christ's our anchor.

### We Are Valuable

What's the most expensive piece of jewelry you own?

When John asked me to marry him, we couldn't afford a big diamond, and we didn't want to start off our marriage with debt just for me to have a fancy rock. At first I thought John might not even buy me an engagement ring but only buy me a wedding band. When he handed me the small box that enclosed the engagement ring, I was absolutely giddy. It didn't matter to me that the diamond wasn't the biggest. It meant the world because I knew John had saved up his money to honor me with the ring.

Even though that was a beautiful experience in my life, that is nothing compared to how God sees us. The biggest, most expensive diamond in the world can't touch what our worth is to our Heavenly Father.

> *Are not five sparrows sold for two pennies? And not one of them is forgotten before God. Why, even the hairs of your head are all numbered. Fear not; you are of more value than many sparrows.*
>
> Luke 12:6–7

Sometimes when we feel rejected, we lose sight of our value. We struggle to find our worth. But that is one of the greatest lies we can believe. Because God sees our potential. He doesn't care how many times we've fallen or how many people dislike us. None of that changes His opinion of us.

And if God thinks we're valuable, it's time we start believing it, too.

# CHAPTER SIXTEEN

## *Breaking Free:*
## *The Truth about Our Savior*

God is sovereign. He cannot fail, and He cannot lie. He is truth, goodness, mercy, hope, love, and He desires us to be set free from the bondage of rejection.

So why are we still in these chains?

Think of it this way: if we sliced our hand open and needed stitches, and we knew about this fantastic doctor who was open 24 hours a day/seven days a week, and he just happened to be next door, would we stand on his front porch and bleed to death because we felt uncomfortable asking him to help?

There is nothing too hard for God. Not your circumstances nor mine. If we are still in chains, it's because we have yet to ask God for help *and* to listen to and heed His direction, or because we do not believe He is who He says He is and that He will do what He says He will do.

So we try to handle our problems alone. We try to deal with the pain of rejection on our own terms. We ignore the One who can help.

We have to stop pretending that we don't need God. We have to take Him out of the box we placed Him in and let Him reign in our lives. Why?

Because He is the only one who can break our chains.

- *I can do this on my own.* How's that working out for you?
- *I've trusted God before, and He let me down.* Did He let you down, or did He give you an answer that you didn't like? Did you grow impatient waiting on Him?

## God Is Our Everything

When we feel rejected, what do we need? To be consoled? Listened to? Loved? Valued? Appreciated? Whatever we need, God is our all in all. That means that He can be our helper, our confidante, our friend, our father. The list goes on.

The Bible has hundreds of descriptions for God. Here's a small portion of them:

- The rose of Sharon
- The lily of the valley
- My defense
- My protector
- My healer
- My salvation
- The Alpha and Omega
- The king of kings
- The prince of peace
- Heavenly Father
- Comforter
- Creator

- Faithful witness
- Friend
- The rock
- The lover of my soul
- The firm foundation
- The everlasting God

*Surely one of those descriptions can fit the bill.*

We need to look no further than God. He is the answer that we've been searching for.

**God Knows Our Pain**

> *For we have not an high priest which cannot be touched with the feeling of our infirmities; but was in all points tempted like as we are, yet without sin.*
> *Hebrews 4:15*

He's been rejected, too. Jesus suffered and died at the hands of those He tried to help. Even his disciples scattered and fled, too afraid to stand by his side. The Bible says that Jesus *endured* the cross. That means He didn't have to go through the agony of the cross. He could have stepped down at any moment. He could have called the host of heaven to come and deliver Him.

Today, people continue to reject the Savior. Many take his name in vain. Others mock Him or those who follow Him. We are not alone in our rejection, if for no other reason than our Savior walked through rejection, too.

He understands what we are going through, but He also knows his plan for our life will still happen regardless of the rejection. Jesus endured the rejection of the cross, but God's ultimate purpose used that pain to usher in the greatest miracle of all time: the resurrection.

God can take whatever mess we're in and still create a miracle.

### God Is Already Victorious

God knows the end from the beginning. He wins. And He's invited us to be victorious through Him.

> *For whatsoever is born of God overcometh the world: and this is the victory that overcometh the world, even our faith.*
> *I John 5:4*

### God Isn't Wrong about Us

The truth about our Savior is that He is never wrong. He sees value in us, therefore there is value in us. He sees beauty, therefore there is. If God is not wrong, then how does He see us?

- We are fearfully and wonderfully made.

> *For thou hast possessed my reins: thou hast covered me in my mother's womb.*
> *I will praise thee; for I am fearfully and wonderfully made:*
> *Psalm 139:13*

- We are priceless.

> *For we are God's handiwork ...*
> *Ephesians 2:10*

- We are blessed.

> *And all these blessings shall come on thee, and overtake thee, if thou shalt hearken unto the voice of the LORD thy God.*
>
> *Blessed shalt thou be in the city, and blessed shalt thou be in the field. Blessed shall be the fruit of thy body, and the fruit of thy ground, and the fruit of thy cattle, the increase of thy kine, and the flocks of thy sheep. Blessed shall be thy basket and thy store. Blessed shalt thou be when thou comest in, and blessed shalt thou be when thou goest out.*
>
> *Deuteronomy 28:2–6*

- We are loved.

> *For I am persuaded, that neither death, nor life, nor angels, nor principalities, nor powers, nor things present, nor things to come, Nor height, nor depth, nor any other creature, shall be able to separate us from the love of God, which is in Christ Jesus our Lord.*
> *Romans 8: 38–39*

- We are daughters of the King of Kings.

> *But as many as received him, to them gave he power to become the sons [daughters] of God,even to them that believe on his name:*
> *John 1:12*

- We are heirs to the throne.

> *That being justified by his grace, we should be*
> *made heirs according to the hope of eternal life.*
> *Titus 3:7*

- We are beautiful.

> *Thou art all fair, my love; there is no spot in thee.*
> *Song of Solomon 4:7*

- We are redeemed.

> *For by grace are ye saved through faith; and that*
> *not of yourselves: it is the gift of God:*
> *Ephesians 2:8*

- Therefore, we are worth it.

> *The LORD hath appeared of old unto me, saying,*
> *Yea, I have loved thee with an everlasting love:*
> *therefore with loving kindness have I drawn thee.*
> *Jeremiah 31:3*

I take comfort in knowing that the God of the universe loves me, finds value in me, and has an amazing plan for my life. So if you are feeling overwhelmed by rejection and the negative emotions that come with it, turn your attention on the one who is ever faithful and who always believes in you.

Believing in Christ is the biggest step we need to take. By turning to Him and handing over control, we will experience freedom in an awe-inspiring, supernatural way.

So what are you waiting for? Go on make the leap. And say good-bye to the chains of rejection.

# Epilogue

## *My Prayer for You*

I wrote this book for you.

I wrote this book for every one of us women who has felt the sting of rejection.

For years I allowed the rejection to consume me. The pain and anguish that dwelled inside affected my life on the outside. Until I gave it to God. I gave Him all of the hurt, all of the betrayal, all of the bitterness, and I asked Him to help me not be ruled by rejection. I asked Him to remind me of my value and worth in His eyes.

My transformation didn't happen overnight. But I started pursuing my relationship with Jesus first and foremost. I began studying the Bible and learning about Biblical characters who struggled just like me. I took time every single day—in the mornings with my coffee and my Bible—to seek Him and find His strength. I'm telling you this important step made all the difference.

As I drew closer to God, He began to gently work on me. He reminded me that I did not need the approval of others to have His. That I did not need to be popular for my purpose to be fulfilled. He opened my eyes to the wonderful people who loved and supported me in my life. In the grand scheme of things, I saw that my "enemies" were really few and far between. Even at work, God showed me how I was actually surrounded by friends who appreciated and valued me and my contributions, and these friends needed my encouragement, too, not just my complaints. He showed me how much He loves me by revealing all He had done for me. From my husband, to my children, to my home, to my health, to my close friends. I began to feel so overwhelmed by His goodness that I started jotting down all the things I was grateful for. It was an epiphany.

The entire time I had been wrapped up in negative emotions and feeling sorry for myself because of rejection, I had been surrounded by the blessings of God. I remember the morning when this realization hit me. I repented right then and there, removed myself from the throne of my heart, and set Jesus there instead. I stopped being consumed by circumstances outside of my control. Instead I asked God to help me be the best *me* I could be.

I am still a work-in-progress, but God set me free from the bondage of rejection. All glory and honor belong to Him.

And He wants the same for you.

*Dear Heavenly Father,*

*So many of my sisters are hurting. They are overwhelmed by rejection and struggle to find their worth. I pray for their complete healing. I pray they will turn to you, because in doing so they will find all the strength, peace, and joy that they need. Convict them in the areas of their life where they need to change and grow, while releasing them from the burden of guilt for things outside of their control. I pray that they find in you all that they need.*

*Set them free, Lord, and order their steps toward their purpose and destiny in you.*

*I ask all these things according to your will.*

*In Jesus' name,*
*Amen*

# Acknowledgements

There are so many people who have blessed me and have been a source of strength in so many ways that I don't know if I can fit them all here. However, I believe I need to give honor where it is due, so I will try!

First of all, thank you, Lord, for being my closest friend and for sticking by my side even in my darkest hours. I love you first and foremost. Thank you for this opportunity to share my testimony with others.

A special thank you to my family. My husband, John, has stuck by me through thick and thin and has believed in my dream right beside me. My sons, Jonathan and Benjamin, are constant reminders of the goodness of God, not to mention I appreciate that they let me write and talk about my writing!

I give honor to my mother and father for raising me in church and for praying for me. Even though my mother is gone from this life, my father has been such a blessing to me and my family, and I am very grateful for it.

Thanks to my siblings: Tonya, Paul, and Sarah. I love you all very much, and I am thankful for your encouragement and prayers. I am proud and thankful to be your sister.

Rachel Anderson, you've been such a blessing. Your friendship was a God-send, and I thank Him for you. You have read my books, critiqued them, shared your books, reminded me what writing was all about, and have just been there when I needed a friend to listen. You are my writing buddy and I appreciate you!

My writing community deserves a big thank you as well. I have so many kindred spirits in all of you, and I love you all to pieces. Thanks for believing in me and helping me become the best writer I can be!

CrossLink Publishing took a chance with me, an author with barely a platform, and I am overwhelmed with gratitude. Thank you for allowing me to have the opportunity to share this book with others.

Lastly, to every single person who has impacted my life, from my students to my colleagues to my church friends to my extended family members, I am who I am because of all of you. I pray God richly blesses and keeps you.

A heartfelt THANK YOU!

# End Notes

1. Anderson, Eric. "Five Myths about Cheating." The Washington Post. (February 13, 2012). www. washingtonpost.com/opinions/five-myths-about-cheating/2012/02/08/gIQANGdaBR_story.html

2. Borboa, Michele, MS. "Why Women Aren't Happy." Sheknows. (Aug. 19, 2012). www.sheknows.com/health-and-wellness/articles/968605/why-women-arent-happy

3. Borzelleca, Daniel. "The Male-Female Ratio in College." Forbes. (February 16, 2012). www.forbes. com/sites/ccap/2012/02/16/the-male-female-ratio-in-college/#b549b9815250

4. Brooks, Chad. "Employees Reveal Why They Hate Their Bosses." Business News Daily. (February 14, 2012). www. businessnewsdaily.com/2024-hate-bosses-bad-listeners. htmo#sthash.i0OWK86T.dpuf

5. Burton, Neel, MD. "The 7 Reasons Why Depression Is More Common in Women." Psychology Today. www. psychologytoday.com/blog/hide-and-seek/201205/the-7-reasons-why-depression-is-more-common-in-women

6. "Cohabitation vs. Marriage: How Love's Choices Shape Life Outcomes." FamilyFacts.org. www.familyfacts.org/

briefs/9/cohabitation-vs-marriage-how-loves-choices-shape-life-outcomes

7. "Depression in Women." Mental Health America. www.mentalhealthamerica.net/conditions/depression-women

8. Grohol, John M. PsyD. "How Common Is Cheating and Infidelity Really?" World of Psychology. (March 22, 2013). www.psychcentral.com/blog/archive/2013/03/22/how-common-is-cheating-infidelity-really/

9. Hollingsworth, Barbara. "Bachelor Nation: 70 percent of Men Aged 20–34 Are Not Married." CNS News. (February 12, 2015). www.cnsnews.com/news/article/barbar-hollingsworth/bachelor-nation-70-men-aged-20-34-are-not-married

10. Livingston, Gretchen. "Fewer Than Half of U.S. Kids Today Live in a Traditional Family. Pew Research Center. (December 22, 2104). www.pewresearch.org/fact-tank/2014/12/22/less-than-half-of-u-s-kids-tody-live-in-a-traditional-family

11. Markey, Dell. "Why Do Teenagers Need Their Fathers?" Global Post. (2016). http://everydaylife.globalpost.com/teenagers-need-fathers-10615.html

12. Mather, Mark. "U.S. Children in Single-Mother Families." Population Reference Bureau. (May 2010). www.prb.org/Publications/Reports/2010/singlemotherfamilies.aspx

13. McGolerick, Elizabeth Weiss. "The Importance of the Father-Daughter Relationship." Sheknows. (October 11, 2012). www.sheknowscom/parenting/articles/821928/the-importance-of-the-father-daughter-relationship

14. Newport, Frank. "Frequent Church Attendance Highest in Utah, Lowest in Vermont." Gallup. (February 17, 2015). www.gallup.com/poll/181601/frequent-church-attendance-highest-utah-lowest-vermont.aspx

15. Nielsen, Linda. "How Dads Affect Their Daughters into Adulthood."InstituteforFamilyStudies.(June3,2014).http://family-studies.org/how-dads-affect-their-daughters-into-adulthood/

16. Paulson, Michael. "Americans Claim to Attend Church Much More Than They Do." The New York Times. (May 17, 2014). www.nytimes.com/2014/05/18/upshot/Americans-claim-to-attend-church-much-more-than-they-do.html?r=0

17. Sherwood, Harriet. "Dying for Christianity: Millions at Risk amid Rise in Persecution across the Globe." The Guardian. (July 27, 2015). www.theguardian.com/world/2015/jul/27/dying-for-chirstianity-millions-at-risk-amid-rise-in-persecution-across-the-globe

18. Stebner, Beth. "Workplace Morale Heads Down: 70 percent of Americans Negative about Their Jobs, Gallup Study Shows." NY Daily News. (June 24, 2013). www.nydailynews.com/news/national/70-u-s-workers-hate-job-poll-article-1.1381297

19. "The Harried Life of the Working Mother." Pew Research Center. (October 1, 2009). www.pewsocialtrends.org/2009/10/01/the-harried-life-of-the-working-mother

20. "The Number of U.S. Children Living in Single-Parent Homes Has Nearly Doubled in 50 Years: Census Data." LifeSite. (January 4, 2013). www.lifesitenews.com/news/the-number-of-children-living-in-single-parent-homes-has-nearly-doubled-in

21. "Unilateral No-Fault Divorce." DivorceResistance.info. http://divorceresistance.info/no_fault.html

22. Weber, Jill, PhD. "Women Bullying Women." Healthy Living. http://www.healthylivingmagazine.us/Articles/85/

23. Weir, Kirsten. "The Pain of Social Rejection." American Psychological Association. (April 2012). http://www.apa.org/monitor/2012/04/rejection.aspx

24. "Women and Depression." American Psychological Association. (2016). Vol. 43, No. 4. www.apa.org/about/gr/issues/women/depression.aspx

25. Zaimov, Stoyan. "Over 100 Million Christians Are Being Persecuted for Their Faith in Jesus Christ, Says Christian Charity Report." CP World. (July 31, 2015). www.christianpost.com/new/over-100-million-christians-are-being-persecuted-for-their-faith-in-jesus-christ-says-christian-charity-report-142144/